STEPHEN HAWKING

GREAT ACHIEVERS:

LIVES OF THE PHYSICALLY CHALLENGED

STEPHEN HAWKING

REVOLUTIONARY PHYSICIST

Melissa McDaniel

Chelsea House Publishers

New York • Philadelphia

CHELSEA HOUSE PUBLISHERS

EDITORIAL DIRECTOR   Richard Rennert
EXECUTIVE MANAGING EDITOR   Karyn Gullen Browne
COPY CHIEF   Robin James
PICTURE EDITOR   Adrian G. Allen
ART DIRECTOR   Robert Mitchell
MANUFACTURING DIRECTOR   Gerald Levine
PRODUCTION COORDINATOR   Marie Claire Cebrián-Ume

GREAT ACHIEVERS: LIVES OF THE PHYSICALLY CHALLENGED

SENIOR EDITOR   Kathy Kuhtz Campbell
SERIES DESIGN   Basia Niemczyc

Staff for STEPHEN HAWKING
EDITORIAL ASSISTANT   Kelsey Goss
PICTURE RESEARCHER   Pat Burns
COVER ILLUSTRATION   Alex Zwarenstein

First Printing

1 3 5 7 9 8 6 4 2

Library of Congress Cataloging-in-Publication Data

McDaniel, Melissa.
Stephen Hawking / Melissa McDaniel.
p. cm.—(Great achievers)
Includes bibliographical references and index.
Summary: Describes the life of the renowned theoretical physicist who has taken the study of cosmology further than most in his field, despite his need for wheelchair and computer to travel and communicate.
ISBN 0-7910-2078-9
     0-7910-2091-6 (pbk.)
1. Hawking, S. W. (Stephen W.)—Juvenile literature. 2. Physicists—Great Britain—Biography—Juvenile literature. [1. Hawking, S. W. (Stephen W.) 2. Physicists. 3. Physically handicapped.] I. Title. II. Series: Great achievers (Chelsea House Publishers)
QC16.H33M33 1994   93-4832
530'.092—dc20   CIP
[B]   AC

FRONTIS:
Stephen Hawking was born on the 300th anniversary of Galileo Galilei's death and holds Sir Isaac Newton's chair as Lucasian Professor of Mathematics at Cambridge University.

CONTENTS

GREAT ACHIEVERS

LIVES OF THE PHYSICALLY CHALLENGED

JIM ABBOTT
baseball star

LUDWIG VAN BEETHOVEN
composer

LOUIS BRAILLE
inventor

CHRIS BURKE
actor

JULIUS CAESAR
Roman emperor

ROY CAMPANELLA
baseball star

RAY CHARLES
musician

ROBERT DOLE
politician

STEPHEN HAWKING
physicist

HELEN KELLER
humanitarian

JACKIE JOYNER-KERSEE
champion athlete

RON KOVIC
antiwar activist

MARIO LEMIEUX
ice hockey star

MARLEE MATLIN
actress

JOHN MILTON
poet

MARY TYLER MOORE
actress

FLANNERY O'CONNOR
author

ITZHAK PERLMAN
violinist

FRANKLIN D. ROOSEVELT
U.S. president

HENRI DE TOULOUSE-LAUTREC
artist

STEVIE WONDER
musician

A MESSAGE FOR EVERYONE

Jerry Lewis

Just 44 years ago—when I was the ripe old age of 23—an incredible stroke of fate rocketed me to overnight stardom as an entertainer. After the initial shock wore off, I began to have a very strong feeling that, in return for all life had given me, I must find a way of giving something back. At just that moment, a deeply moving experience in my personal life persuaded me to take up the leadership of a fledgling battle to defeat a then little-known group of diseases called muscular dystrophy, as well as other related neuromuscular diseases—all of which are disabling and, in the worst cases, cut life short.

In 1950, when the Muscular Dystrophy Association (MDA)—of which I am national chairman—was established, physical disability was looked on as a matter of shame. Franklin Roosevelt, who guided America through World War II from a wheelchair, and Harold Russell, the World War II hero who lost both hands in battle, then became an Academy Award–winning movie star and chairman of the President's Committee on Employment of the Handicapped, were the exceptions. One of the reasons that muscular dystrophy and related diseases were so little known was that people who had been disabled by them were hidden at home, away from the pity and discomfort with which they were generally regarded by society. As I got to know and began working with people who have disabilities, I quickly learned what a tragic mistake this perception was. And my determination to correct this terrible problem soon became as great as my commitment to see disabling neuromuscular diseases wiped from the face of the earth.

I have long wondered why it never occurs to us, as we experience the knee-jerk inclination to feel sorry for people who are physically disabled, that lives such as those led by President Roosevelt, Harold Russell, and all of the extraordinary people profiled in this Great Achievers series demonstrate unmistakably how wrong we are. Physical disability need not be something that blights life and destroys opportunity for personal fulfillment and accomplishment. On the contrary, as people such as Ray Charles, Stephen Hawking, and Ron Kovic prove, physical disability can be a spur to greatness rather than a condemnation of emptiness.

In fact, if my experience with physically disabled people can be taken as a guide, as far as accomplishment is concerned, they have a slight edge on the rest of us. The unusual challenges they face require finding greater-than-average sources of energy and determination to achieve much of what able-bodied people take for granted. Often, this ultimately translates into a lifetime of superior performance in whatever endeavor people with disabilities choose to pursue.

If you have watched my Labor Day Telethon over the years, you know exactly what I am talking about. Annually, we introduce to tens of millions of Americans people whose accomplishments would distinguish them regardless of their physical conditions—top-ranking executives, physicians, scientists, lawyers, musicians, and artists. The message I hope the audience receives is not that these extraordinary individuals have achieved what they have by overcoming a dreadful disadvantage that the rest of us are lucky not to have to endure. Rather, I hope our viewers reflect on the fact that these outstanding people have been ennobled and strengthened by the tremendous challenges they have faced.

In 1992, MDA, which has grown over the past four decades into one of the world's leading voluntary health agencies, established a personal achievement awards program to demonstrate to the nation that the distinctive qualities of people with disabilities are by no means confined to the famous. What could have been more appropriate or timely in that year of the implementation of the 1990 Americans with Disabilities Act than to take an action that could perhaps finally achieve the alteration of public perception of disability, which MDA had struggled over four decades to achieve?

On Labor Day, 1992, it was my privilege to introduce to America MDA's inaugural national personal achievement award winner, Steve Mikita, assistant attorney general of the state of Utah. Steve graduated magna cum laude from Duke University as its first wheelchair student in history and was subsequently named the outstanding young lawyer of the year by the Utah Bar Association. After he spoke on the Telethon with an eloquence that caused phones to light up from coast to coast, people asked me where he had been all this time and why they had not known of him before, so deeply impressed were they by him. I answered that he and thousands like him have been here all along. We just have not adequately *noticed* them.

It is my fervent hope that we can eliminate indifference once and for all and make it possible for all of our fellow citizens with disabilities to gain their rightfully high place in our society.

ON FACING CHALLENGES

John Callahan

I was paralyzed for life in 1972, at the age of 21. A friend and I were driving in a Volkswagen on a hot July night, when he smashed the car at full speed into a utility pole. He suffered only minor injuries. But my spinal cord was severed during the crash, leaving me without any feeling from my diaphragm downward. The only muscles I could move were some in my upper body and arms, and I could also extend my fingers. After spending a lot of time in physical therapy, it became possible for me to grasp a pen.

I've always loved to draw. When I was a kid, I made pictures of everything from Daffy Duck (one of my lifelong role models) to caricatures of my teachers and friends. I've always been a people watcher, it seems; and I've always looked at the world in a sort of skewed way. Everything I see just happens to translate immediately into humor. And so, humor has become my way of coping. As the years have gone by, I have developed a tremendous drive to express my humor by drawing cartoons.

The key to cartooning is to put a different spin on the expected, the normal. And that's one reason why many of my cartoons deal with the disabled: amputees, quadriplegics, paraplegics, the blind. The public is not used to seeing them in cartoons.

But there's another reason why my subjects are often disabled men and women. I'm sick and tired of people who presume to speak for the disabled. Call me a cripple, call me a gimp, call me paralyzed for life.

Just don't call me something I'm not. I'm not "differently abled," and my cartoons show that disabled people should not be treated any differently than anyone else.

All of the men, women, and children who are profiled in the Great Achievers series share this in common: their various handicaps have not prevented them from accomplishing great things. Their life stories are worth knowing about because they have found the strength and courage to develop their talents and to follow their dreams as fully as they can.

Whether able-bodied or disabled, a person must strive to overcome obstacles. There's nothing greater than to see a person who faces challenges and conquers them, regardless of his or her limitations.

By the time he had reached the age of 32, Stephen Hawking, shown here in 1982 in his office in the Department of Applied Mathematics and Theoretical Physics at Cambridge, had already become known as one of the most distinguished cosmologists in the world.

1

BLACK HOLES
ARE NOT BLACK

IN LATE JANUARY 1974, Dennis Sciama, a professor of astrophysics at Oxford University, England, was walking through the halls of the Institute of Astronomy in Cambridge, England, when suddenly Martin Rees, a professor at the institute, came rushing toward him. "Have you heard?" Rees exclaimed, "Stephen's changed everything!"

"What are you talking about?" Sciama asked. With great excitement, Rees told him that Stephen Hawking, a former student of Sciama's, had made a major breakthrough. Sciama had been Hawking's adviser when Hawking was a graduate student in theoretical physics at Cambridge University in the early 1960s. Now, eager to learn the details of Hawking's new discoveries, Sciama hurried off to see him. Their conversation so excited him that he invited Hawking to speak at a conference he was organizing.

Although Hawking had just turned 32, he already had gained a reputation as one of the preeminent cosmologists in the world. Cosmology, the study of the nature and origin of the universe, had only blossomed as a branch of physics in the mid-1960s. It had previously been a backwater of physics because it was based almost entirely on mathematical models rather than on observable phenomena. For this reason, experimental physicists who worked in laboratories were often skeptical of theoretical physicists, such as cosmologists. But during the 1960s, astronomers using improved technology verified some of the predictions cosmologists had made. In the next few years, theoretical physicists made great strides in understanding the universe, and cosmology became a very popular and respected specialty.

Most of Hawking's contributions to cosmology were in the study of black holes, portions of space-time where gravity is so strong that nothing can escape. Physicists surmise that a black hole forms when a star with at least three times the mass of the sun burns off all of its nuclear fuel and collapses in on itself. As gravity pulls all of the matter into a tiny space, any other object that comes near it would also be sucked down into the maelstrom. Because even light cannot elude the gravitational field of this area, it is known as a black hole.

On a chilly February day in 1974, some of the world's foremost physicists gathered for Dennis Sciama's conference at the Rutherford-Appleton Laboratory just outside of Oxford. As one speaker after another delivered lectures announcing their latest findings, Stephen Hawking sat off to the side feeling excited, but also a bit concerned about how his colleagues would react to his work. Many of those present were not cosmologists. In fact, many were not theoretical physicists at all, but instead were experimentalists who worked with particle acceleration or nuclear weapons theory.

In graduate school, Hawking had developed a reputation as someone who would ask penetrating questions at lectures. Although this could be quite embarrassing for some speakers, most established scientists respected him for his discerning mind. For younger scientists, however, his combination of brashness and acute intelligence could be very intimidating. At this conference, his excitement made it difficult for him to concentrate, but, with his usual confidence, he asked incisive questions about his peers' papers while waiting patiently for his turn to speak.

Finally Hawking's turn came. He moved to the front of the room. With his straight brown hair and thin build—he weighed probably no more than 120 pounds—he did not appear to be an imposing figure. But he was already known as a rising star in his field and everyone at the conference sat with rapt attention waiting for him to begin.

The lights went down and slides of equations and diagrams were projected behind Hawking as he began to speak. His voice was virtually incomprehensible to those who did not know him. Since 1963 he had suffered from amyotrophic lateral sclerosis (ALS), known in the United States as Lou Gehrig's disease named after the great New York Yankee baseball player whose career it cut short. ALS is a progressive disease that affects the nerve cells in the spinal cord and parts of the brain, causing loss of control of muscle movement. Although the brain itself is not damaged by ALS, it is no longer able to control and communicate with the body. In spite of the fact that ALS often causes death within three or four years, Hawking had defied the odds.

Hawking had been using a wheelchair since 1970 and his speech was now so slurred that it was sometimes necessary for acquaintances to interpret his words for strangers. To the uninitiated ear, his voice sounded like a rough hum intermingled with many *m*'s and *n*'s. Most of the people in the lecture hall that day, however, knew him

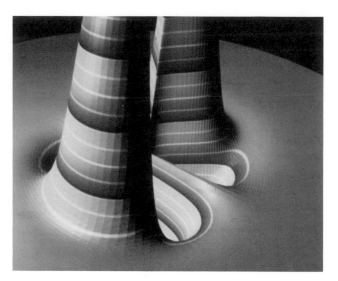

The stills above and opposite show the evolution of a distorted single black hole system. Outgoing radiation is depicted as the flat surface and incoming radiation as the height. The black line denotes the apparent horizon of the black hole. In 1974, Hawking maintained that, contrary to everyone's understanding of physics at the time, black holes—which are believed to be caused by collapsed stars— were not completely black but emitted radiation.

well enough to decipher his words. But they could not believe what they heard. Hawking was claiming that, contrary to everyone's understanding of physics at the time, black holes were not completely black, but they emitted radiation.

When Hawking finished his speech, silence enveloped the room. Too stunned to ask any questions, the audience sat in a hushed quiet, trying to digest his astonishing claim. Finally, John Taylor, the chairman of the meeting and a professor at King's College in London, rose and exclaimed, "You must be wrong, Stephen, I don't believe a word of it!" He and one of his colleagues strode out of the room in a rage. Hawking continued to sit quietly at the podium. He was stunned as well, never having expected such a violent reaction.

Hawking knew that his findings were revolutionary. The ideas in his speech had initially occurred to him one evening a few years earlier when he was getting into bed, which, as he has often stated, is a rather slow process because of his disability. That night Hawking realized that the concept of entropy could be applied to black holes. Entropy is the measure of the amount of disorder in a system. According to the Second Law of Thermo-

dynamics, if something has an entropy, it must have a temperature. When an object has a temperature, it emits radiation—but nothing was supposed to come out of a black hole. Hawking knew he was onto something big. The apparent contradiction of black holes emitting radiation excited him so much that he could hardly sleep that night.

The next morning Hawking set about devising a means by which black holes could have a temperature and radiate heat. For the next three years he struggled with the problem. He still did not believe that it was actually possible for black holes to emit anything. Finally, toward the end of 1973, he discovered a mechanism that would allow black holes to emit particles of radiation. This method relied upon quantum mechanics, the branch of physics that describes the often peculiar behavior of subatomic particles. Quantum mechanics posits the existence of "virtual particles" that cannot be detected but that have a measurable effect. Virtual particles and antiparticles are created in pairs, but they immediately collide and annihilate one another. Hawking determined that if one of these pairs materialized right at the event horizon, the boundary of a black hole, it was possible for one of the particles to fall into the black hole. Because the remaining particle had no partner to annihilate it, it would be able to escape. The particle that got away would take the form of radiation. According to Albert Einstein's theory of general relativity, which explains gravity's effect on very large objects, nothing is supposed to escape from a black hole. Hawking, however, had shown that black holes are not black; instead they radiate what was known from then on as Hawking radiation.

Immediately following the conference where Hawking had dropped his bombshell, John Taylor, the scientist who denounced Hawking's speech, wrote a paper criticizing Hawking's findings and submitted it to the scientific journal *Nature*. When the editor of *Nature* asked Hawking what he thought of Taylor's paper, Hawking responded that he thought it should be published. He had no objection to Taylor embarrassing himself by publishing opinions about a subject on which he had done no research.

The published form of Hawking's findings appeared in March 1974. Because of Hawking's disability, writing papers is a more difficult process for him than for other scientists, so he tends to choose his words carefully, resulting in a concise but very elegant style. According to Dennis Sciama, Hawking's paper on black hole radiation was "one of the most beautiful in the history of physics." A few weeks after publication of the paper, physicists all across the world were discussing Hawking radiation. Some claimed that it was the most important advance in theoretical physics in years. After a few months of study, everyone in the scientific community agreed with Hawking's hypothesis. Even John Taylor admitted that Hawking could be right.

The real significance of Hawking's new theory, however, was not just that it advanced the understanding of the nature of black holes, but that it was a first step in the unification of quantum mechanics and general relativity, the two great accomplishments of theoretical physics in the 20th century. Ever since Einstein, theoretical physicists had been searching for one law from which all other laws of physics can be derived. If this "theory of everything," the Grand Unification, is discovered, many people believe it will shed great light on the origins of the universe. Martin Rees has dubbed this search the physicist's Holy Grail. When Hawking discovered a process by which black holes could radiate, he wed general relativity, quantum mechanics, and thermodynamics in a way no one had done before. It was a first step, although a small one, toward a Grand Unification Theory. This great achievement, however, merely whet Stephen Hawking's appetite. He was now on a quest to find the theory to explain all theories.

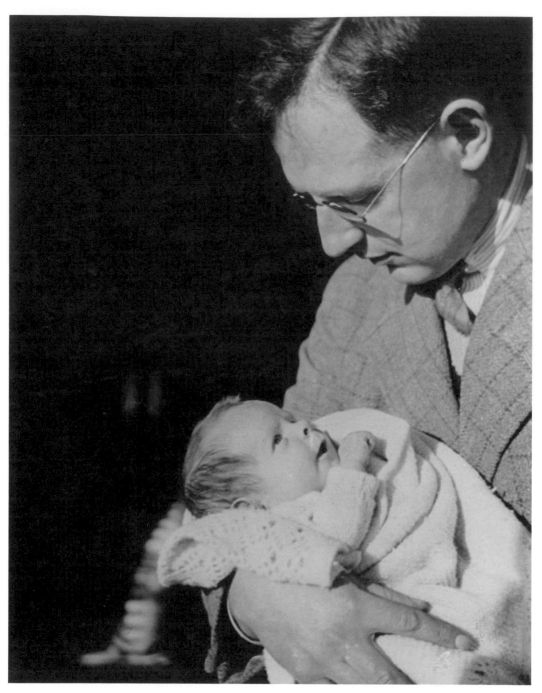

Frank Hawking holds his newborn son, Stephen, in January 1942. Isobel and Frank Hawking, who had both attended Oxford University and were married during the early years of World War II, were considered to be an eccentric but highly intelligent couple.

2

THE YOUNG SCIENTIST

STEPHEN WILLIAM HAWKING was born on January 8, 1942, exactly 300 years after the death of Galileo Galilei, the Italian astronomer whom many call the father of modern science. When Stephen Hawking was born, World War II had been raging in Europe for more than two years. The Germans were bombing all of southern England every night, including Highgate, the London suburb where Hawking's parents, Frank and Isobel, lived. After a bomb fell near the Hawking home, shattering the back windows of the house, they decided that Mrs. Hawking should go to Oxford for the birth of Stephen, their first child. The German and British governments had agreed not to bomb each other's historic universities, and consequently, Cambridge and Oxford in England, and Heidelberg and Göttingen in Germany were spared from destruction. In the short time that Isobel Hawking was awaiting childbirth in Oxford, she bought an astronomical atlas. A relative would later tell her that, "This is a very prophetic thing for you to have done."

Stephen's father, Frank Hawking, was the son of a once-successful Yorkshire farmer who had gone bankrupt during an agricultural depression that hit England in the early part of the 20th century. In spite of their financial difficulties, Frank's parents still managed to send him to Oxford University, where he studied medicine, specializing in tropical diseases. When war broke out in 1939, Dr. Hawking was working in East Africa, but he returned home to England to volunteer for military service. The military, however, believed that he would be more useful

On May 15, 1941, two men survey the damage to the city of London during the German blitzkrieg. Although the Hawkings lived in High-gate, a London suburb, they decided that their first child, Stephen, should be born in the security of the university town of Oxford, which was protected from bombing by a German and British agreement.

to the country by doing research; therefore, he settled in at a medical research institute where he met his future wife. Following the war, Dr. Hawking was appointed head of the Division of Parasitology at the National Institute of Medical Research.

Stephen's mother, Isobel, was the second of seven children of a doctor in Glasgow, Scotland. Although her family was middle class, they, too, scraped together enough money to send her to college at a time when very few women received higher education. She attended Oxford, which had only begun granting degrees to women in 1920, but she did not meet Frank Hawking while she was a student there. After graduation, she worked at several jobs, none of which she liked. The most loathsome of these was as inspector of taxes. She hated the position so much that she quit after a few months to become a secretary at a medical research institute, a job for which she was vastly overqualified. It was there that she met the shy researcher, and the couple married during the early years of the war.

In 1950, the family moved to St. Albans, a small middle-class town north of London. By this time, Stephen had two younger sisters, Mary and Philippa. A younger brother, Edward, was adopted when Stephen was 13. They lived in a rambling old house that had fallen into disrepair. The Hawkings never concerned themselves with the fence that was falling down, the wallpaper that was peeling, or the panes of glass that periodically blew out, never to be replaced. The children were sometimes embarrassed by the house's dismal condition and found it spooky, but they also thought it was a great place for adventure. According to Mary Hawking, Stephen knew 11 ways to get into the house, including climbing up onto the roof and in through a window.

Friends and neighbors in St. Albans thought that the Hawkings were quite eccentric. Every year, Stephen's father traveled to Africa for a few months to do research and then returned with all sorts of strange and wonderful

The Hawkings moved to St. Albans, pictured here, a small town northwest of London, in 1950. The children—Stephen, Mary, Philippa, and Edward—regarded their huge, rickety old house as an adventure. Stephen knew at least 11 ways to enter the house, including climbing up onto the roof and getting in through a window.

objects and carved animals. The house was also filled with books that were stacked two deep in the shelves and covered most of the available horizontal surfaces. Basil King, a childhood friend of Stephen's, remembers that at dinners in the Hawking home, Stephen would talk to him, "but the rest of the family would be sitting at the table reading a book—a behavior which was not really approved of in my circle, but which was tolerated from the Hawkings because they were recognized to be very eccentric, highly intelligent, very clever people—but still a bit odd." Frank Hawking had a noticeable stutter and many other members of the family often stammered when they spoke. According to Basil King, many of Stephen's friends believed that "the Hawkings were so clever that their speech couldn't keep up with their thoughts; that's why they stuttered, why they stumbled, why they ran over themselves in this rather clumsy form of speaking." Their eccentric reputation was augmented by the succession of old taxis that they owned at a time when very few families owned cars at all. The Hawkings would drive to the country in a huge open-air taxi, the children sitting in the back playing cards at a folding table.

The combination of Frank Hawking's inherent shyness and his frequent trips abroad made him a rather remote figure. Even when he was in England, he often thought more about his work and how to provide for his family on a fairly small income than about his children. He did, however, introduce Stephen to astronomy. The whole family would lie on the ground, gazing through a telescope up at the stars. Isobel Hawking could see Stephen's interest in the stars, noting that he always had the greatest sense of

Young Stephen holds the boom line of a sailboat. Hawking was a small, awkward boy, full of ingenuity, and he spoke in fits and starts, just like his father. Stephen's friends called his manner of speaking Hawkingese.

wonder. Her husband and Stephen also made fireworks together, combining chemicals to produce different colors.

Isobel Hawking was a warmer figure than her husband, more actively involved with her children and their friends. She was also very interested in politics. Like many English intellectuals, she had been a member of the Communist party during the 1930s. By the 1950s, she belonged to the Labour party and was active in the Campaign for Nuclear Disarmament. She often went to demonstrations and encouraged Stephen to join her. Stephen absorbed her political influence, and his political sympathies would always remain with the Labour party.

Because social status was very important in England, Frank Hawking was quite concerned about where Stephen attended school. Although Dr. Hawking had gone to a small private school, he firmly believed that his career had been hampered because he had not attended a more prestigious school. He did not want Stephen to have to face the same obstacles, so he decided to send him to Westminster School in London, one of the most distinguished private schools in the country. But Dr. Hawking did not earn enough money to afford tuition at Westminster; consequently, Stephen needed to win a scholarship. Unfortunately, on the day of the scholarship examination, Stephen became ill. Disappointed, his father enrolled him at the St. Albans School, an academically strong school affiliated with the local cathedral.

When Stephen entered St. Albans, he was a small, awkward boy, full of imagination and energy, and always very messy. Like his father, he spoke in fits and starts in a way that his friends dubbed "Hawkingese." In his first year at St. Albans, he came in third from the bottom of his class. When his mother asked him why he did so poorly, he nonchalantly responded that many other students had not done much better. His teachers always recognized that he was intelligent, however, and by his third year at St. Albans his studies had improved and he was part of the

top group of students. Still, he was not seen as the most intelligent of what was, in fact, a remarkably smart group of boys that became his circle of friends.

Stephen's friends took an early interest in board games. The Hawkings owned Monopoly, but the boys quickly grew tired of it and began to modify it. Soon they had railways running across the board. But even this was not complicated enough for them, so Stephen began devising his own games. Most of these were war games for which Stephen would make up the rules and laws, and his friend Roger Ferneyhaugh, who had an artistic bent, would construct boards and playing pieces. Typically, the games would last four or five hours, but some of them would go on for a week. Hawking's most elaborate concoction was the Feudal Game, which was based upon the social and

Stephen goes riding while on holiday. Even before Stephen became a teenager, he was already judged by his friends to be brilliant. In 1954, during a discussion with Hawking about religion and philosophy, one friend recalled, "It was at this point that I realized for the first time that he was in some way different and not just bright, not just clever, not just original, but exceptional."

political world of medieval England. The rules were so intricate that it often took a whole evening to determine the outcome of one roll of the dice. Michael Church, a member of the group, recalled that Stephen "loved the fact that he had created the world and then created the laws that governed it. And that he was causing us to obey those laws."

By the end of 1954, the group's attention had turned to religion. Instead of playing games, they would gather to discuss faith, God, and their place in the world. Although Stephen had already won the divinity prize at school and was thoroughly knowledgeable about the Bible, he remained somewhat aloof from this craze. As a budding scientist, he was too much of a rationalist to become actively involved in this overtly emotional endeavor. It was at about this time that some of the other boys realized that Stephen's intelligence was different from theirs. Michael Church remembers discussing the meaning of life and suddenly becoming "aware that he was egging me on, leading me to make a fool of myself. . . . I felt looked down upon from a great height. . . . It was at this point that I realized for the first time that he was in some way different and not just bright, not just clever, not just original, but exceptional. And there was some overarching arrogance, if you like, some overarching sense of what the world was about."

For a brief time the boys became fascinated by extrasensory perception (ESP), which Stephen thought was grounded more in science than Christianity was. He believed that it was possible to prove or disprove the existence of ESP, so Stephen and his friends did experiments to try to control the roll of dice with their minds. His interest in ESP evaporated, however, after attending a lecture that showed that whenever ESP experiments obtained good results, the experimental methods had invariably been faulty, and that when the scientific technique was rigorous, there were no results. Although Stephen was still quite young, his logical mind demanded the rationality and proof that neither religion nor ESP could offer.

Ever since Stephen was about nine, he knew that he wanted to be a scientist. He loved to find out how things worked, often taking apart clocks and radios to see their inner workings. Unfortunately, he was seldom able to put them back together. His room was a veritable mad scientist's laboratory, filled with test tubes, various electrical devices, and debris from old models. Already he had intuitive insight into math and physics, often getting excellent grades on homework on which he spent very little time. A friend recalled that, "While I would be worrying away at a complicated mathematical solution to a problem, *he just knew the answer*—he didn't have to think about it."

His scientific instincts soon attracted him to computers, which in the late 1950s were virtually unknown. In Britain, only a few universities and the government possessed them. But in 1958, Stephen and his friends built a computer, albeit a very primitive one, made out of the insides of clocks and an old telephone switchboard. Stephen was one of the primary designers of the computer, but he was unable to do much of the building because he was never very coordinated with his hands. After a month of soldering and resoldering, the machine, which the boys called the Logical Uniselector Computing Engine (LUCE), finally worked. Although LUCE could only give an answer if it was asked the right sort of mathematical question, the boys received a lot of attention for their invention. The *Herts Advertiser*, the local newspaper, published a story about the schoolboys who built an amazing new machine. The following year, Stephen's last year at St. Albans, the boys built a more sophisticated version of LUCE that was supposed to "actually do sums." Many years later, the new head of computing at St. Albans School found a box marked "LUCE" under a table. Thinking it was old junk, a pile of transistors and wires, he threw the box in the trash. Subsequently, he realized that he had thrown away the computer that Stephen Hawking had built.

For much of Stephen's last year at St. Albans, he and his father had been arguing over what he should study in college. Stephen wanted to take mathematics and physics, whereas his father wanted him to follow in his footsteps and study medicine. Stephen was not interested in biology, however, believing that it was too "descriptive." Math and physics were more fundamental, he felt, and could lead to the underlying truths about the natural world. His father argued that the only job in mathematics was that of teaching. Besides, Frank Hawking was eager to see his son attend University College at Oxford, where he had gone to school, and it did not offer a course of study in mathematics. But Stephen knew what he wanted. Finally they com-

This aerial view of Oxford University depicts Christ Church College (the domed tower, center). Oxford comprises 35 colleges, one of which is University College, Frank Hawking's alma mater and the school that offered 17-year-old Stephen a scholarship.

promised, with Stephen agreeing to study chemistry, physics, and mathematics. This was acceptable to Stephen because he was most interested in physics, believing that mathematics was primarily a tool for doing physics. With the decision made, Stephen prepared to take the entrance examinations for Oxford University.

Oxford University comprises 35 colleges, one of which is Frank Hawking's alma mater, University College. Dr. Hawking was very ambitious and he desperately wanted Stephen to be awarded one of the scholarships that was distributed based upon the results of entrance examinations. A scholarship would not only pay a portion of the cost of attending school, but was also very prestigious and brought with it special privileges. Although he knew that his son was bright, Dr. Hawking was not confident that Stephen would be awarded a scholarship to University College, and, therefore, he decided to visit Dr. Robert Berman, the professor who would be Stephen's tutor if he was accepted. Dr. Berman did not appreciate the kind of pressure that Dr. Hawking was placing on him. Stephen performed so well on his $12\frac{1}{2}$ hours of written exams, however, that Berman did not hold Dr. Hawking's pushiness against Stephen. As part of the entrance exam, Stephen had to be interviewed by a panel of the university's faculty and then by Dr. Berman alone, to whom he had to demonstrate his knowledge of physics.

Following this rigorous testing, Stephen retreated to St. Albans to await his fate. After 10 days, he received a letter asking him to return for another interview. This was heartening news because it meant that the school was considering him very seriously. Only later would Stephen learn that he had scored 95 percent on his physics exams and only slightly lower on the others. Shortly after the second interview, University College offered him a scholarship. In October 1959, at the age of 17, Stephen Hawking made his way to Oxford.

Hawking, photographed here as an undergraduate, found the transition to college life difficult. He was lonely and bored with his academic studies.

3

LAZY DAYS
AND ADVERSITY

THE CITY OF OXFORD lies about 50 miles northwest of London and is situated between the Thames and Cherwell rivers. The various colleges of Oxford University are scattered throughout the town. University College, which Hawking would attend, is in the center of town. Founded in 1249, it is the oldest college in Oxford. Although most of the students at Oxford in 1959 had gone to the country's premier private schools, the number of students from middle-class and working-class backgrounds was increasing. The division between the classes was still very much intact, however, and the privileged students very rarely mingled with those of more modest means.

The transition to college life was difficult for Stephen Hawking. None of his friends went to Oxford, and many of the students there were older than he was, having already completed military service. He was lonely and bored. The academic system at Oxford did little to

University College, located in the center of town, was founded in 1249 and is the oldest college in Oxford. Hawking later said that the prevailing attitude while he attended Oxford was "very anti-work. . . . You were supposed either to be brilliant without effort or to accept your limitations and get a fourth-class degree . . . to work hard . . . was regarded as the mark of a grey man, the worst epithet in the Oxford vocabulary."

alleviate Hawking's boredom. Students were supposed to attend several lectures each week as well as a tutorial in which they would discuss problems that had been assigned the previous week. The only exams that mattered in terms of getting a degree were the finals that the students took at the end of their first and third years. The attitude at Oxford at that time was, according to Hawking, "very anti-work." "You were supposed either to be brilliant without effort or to accept your limitations and get a fourth-class degree. To work hard to get a better class of degree was regarded as the mark of a grey man, the worst epithet in the Oxford vocabulary." For Hawking, the work was so simple that he easily fell into the first category. He estimates that he studied only about 1,000 hours in his three years at Oxford, an average of 1 hour per day.

With Hawking's intuitive understanding of math and physics, he seldom had trouble doing any of the work. One week, Dr. Berman gave his four physics students 13 problems to do. They were supposed to answer as many as they could for the next week's class. On the day of the tutorial the following week, the other three students encountered Hawking at about nine in the morning and asked him how many problems he had done. When he responded that he had not even tried them yet, the other students laughed. Working the whole week, two of them together had managed to do one and a half problems, whereas the other student working alone had completed but one. While the others went to the lectures that they were all supposed to attend, Hawking went to his room to work on the physics problems. At about noon, the other physics students met Hawking on the way to the tutorial. "Ah, Hawking," one of them said, "How many have you managed to do then?"

"Well," Hawking said, "I've only had time to do the first ten." The others began to laugh until they realized that Hawking was serious. One of the other students, Derek Powney, recalls that "I think at that point we realized that it was not just that we weren't in the same street, we weren't on the same planet."

Hawking seldom took notes in class, had few books, and sometimes let his lack of interest in school turn into open disdain. When given a textbook on statistical physics and told to answer a set of problems, he returned the next week with no problems done, but with every error in the textbook marked. After discussing the errors in the textbook for 20 minutes, the tutor realized that Hawking knew much more about the subject than he did. According to his adviser, Robert Berman, "Undergraduate physics was simply not a challenge for him. He did very little work, really, because anything that was do-able he could do. It was only necessary for him to know something could be done, and he could do it without looking to see how other people did it."

In the middle of Hawking's second year at Oxford, his boredom finally dissipated. Although the work was still much too simple for him, he had discovered a diversion— rowing. Rowing is taken very seriously at Oxford, and those who do it are often up at the crack of dawn, even in the freezing weather, to do exercises and attend early practices. Although oarsmen are usually large, muscular people, the coxswain who steers the boat should be a small man who will not weigh the boat down. Hawking's small size made him well suited to coxing. He also had a loud voice so he could easily be heard by the oarsmen as they were gliding up and down the river. Hawking was an adventurous coxswain who often tried to steer his boat through such narrow spaces that, when he returned it to shore, bits of the boat would be broken off.

Hawking (far right) became a coxswain, the steersman of a racing shell who usually directs the crew, during his second year at Oxford. He loved rowing and it enabled him to become part of a socially acceptable crowd.

Hawking loved rowing. Not only was it a tremendous amount of fun, but it made him part of a socially acceptable crowd. No longer was he the gawky, awkward, lonely genius. Instead he was a member of the boating crowd who drank a lot of ale, were very fit, and lived life to the fullest. For the skinny boy who had never been good at sports or good with his hands, it was an amazing transformation. Although he was supposed to be in physics lab three days a week, from nine in the morning until three in the afternoon, he was absolutely committed to being on the river every afternoon. He and his fellow physics student and rower, Gordon Berry, became adept at collecting data very quickly. Although they gathered only a minimal amount of data, they did the maximum amount of analysis so that it looked as though they had actually done the experiment. Somehow they convinced the tutors, who knew they had not been at the lab, that they had done the entire experiment. Berry recalled, "We were never cheating, but there was a lot of interpretation going on."

Toward the end of Hawking's third year, looming finals forced him to think more about school. The final exams, which lasted four days, had a wide range of questions from which the students could choose. Because Hawking had studied so little, he knew that he would have to avoid the questions that required factual knowledge in favor of those that were more theoretical in nature. These he could answer with his intuitive understanding of physics. Each night after exams, the four physics students would gather for dinner, not to discuss the tests, but just for the camaraderie. Hawking became increasingly depressed about the way the tests were going, and by the night before the last exam, he could hardly sleep.

Hawking wanted to go to Cambridge University to do doctoral work, but to be accepted there, he needed a first-class degree, the highest possible of the four levels of degrees bestowed by Oxford. After the tests were over, he was convinced that he had not done well enough and that he would only get a second-class degree. He soon heard that he was on the borderline between a first- and a second-class degree and that he would face an interview to determine which class of degree he would receive.

Although Hawking had a bad reputation among the faculty as being a lazy student who was much more interested in drinking and having fun than in studying, the interview was actually a boon for him. His adviser, Robert Berman, noted that, in person, anyone with any intelligence would soon see that Hawking was far smarter than he or she was. During the interview, the panel asked Hawking what his plans were for the future. He replied that he wanted to do research, and then he said, "If you award me a First, I will go to Cambridge. If I receive a Second, I shall stay in Oxford, so I expect you will give me a First." He turned out to be right. Hawking received his first-class degree and prepared to go to Cambridge in the fall of 1962.

Hawking had long been considering what area of theoretical physics in which to do his doctoral research. His choice came down to cosmology or elementary particles, particles that are so small that they cannot be subdivided any further. He decided that elementary particles were less interesting because they had no overarching theory. Although new particles were being discovered, all that scientists could really do was arrange them into families, a process called classification. Cosmology, on the other hand, had Einstein's general theory of relativity to serve as its theoretical basis. Once Hawking had chosen cosmology as his field, he had no choice but to attend Cambridge rather than staying at Oxford, because Oxford did not offer cosmological research as a course of study.

Cambridge University also appealed to Hawking because Fred Hoyle, the most eminent British astronomer of the time, taught there. Hawking was very excited about having the opportunity to study with Hoyle. When he learned that instead of Hoyle his adviser would be Dennis Sciama, he was very disappointed. Hawking had never

heard of Sciama, but he soon realized that Sciama was an excellent scientist and would make a better adviser than Hoyle—Hoyle frequently traveled, whereas Sciama was usually in Cambridge, ready to help his students.

Just as Hawking had trouble adjusting to life at Oxford, his early time at Cambridge went very badly. His poor study habits came back to haunt him. He soon realized that he had not studied mathematics well enough at Oxford, so now he was having difficulty with the calculations needed for studying general relativity. Although he continued to study very little, his work load was much more demanding than it had been at Oxford. He was having trouble keeping up. Moreover, he was having difficulty finding a research project that was suitable for a doctorate course of study. Even more troublesome, some physical problems that he

Professor Fred Hoyle, the leading British astronomer of the day, taught at Cambridge University when Hawking went there to study cosmology in 1962.

The astrophysicist Dennis Sciama became Hawking's adviser when Hawking entered Cambridge as a graduate student. Although Hawking was initially disappointed that Hoyle would not be his adviser, he soon realized that Sciama was a preeminent scientist who was more accessible to his students.

had noticed, but had ignored, in his last year at Oxford began to worsen.

During his third year at Oxford, Hawking had been getting clumsier. In one frightening incident, he tumbled all the way to the bottom of a flight of stairs and, because of a blow to his head, lost his memory. At first he could not even remember his own name. Gradually, as his friends asked him if he could remember coming to Oxford, then what happened a year ago, then a month ago, his memory returned. It took two hours, but finally he remembered falling down the stairs. Another time, in the midst of a discussion about whether being unable to walk a straight line was a sign of being drunk, Hawking interjected that, because he could never walk a straight line, it was not a legitimate test.

Not until the end of 1962, during his first year at Cambridge when Hawking went back to St. Albans for Christmas vacation, did it become obvious that there was something wrong with his health. At Cambridge, no one had known him long enough to notice his physical decline. Dennis Sciama merely thought that Hawking had a speech impediment. But his family and friends, who had not seen him for months, immediately noticed his clumsiness and awkwardness with his hands. At a New Year's Eve party, Hawking encountered some of his old friends from the St. Albans School. Word had been spreading that he was ill. With a great sense of foreboding, they watched as he tried to pour wine and spilled more of it on the table than into the glasses.

At the party that evening Hawking met Jane Wilde. She was just completing secondary school in St. Albans and was planning to study modern languages at Westfield College in London in the fall. She found Hawking intriguing, and was attracted by his wit, intelligence, and eccentricity. Although she thought Hawking was arrogant, she felt this was mitigated by his uncertainty, his sense that he was not in control of what was happening inside of his body. Hawking, in turn, was attracted by Jane's energy and optimism. Over the next few months, their friendship blossomed.

During the holidays, Hawking's parents finally insisted that he go to see the family doctor. While ice-skating with his mother, he had fallen down and had been unable to stand up again. Their doctor referred him to a specialist. Not long after Hawking's 21st birthday in early 1963, he entered the hospital for tests. The doctors took muscle samples and stuck him with electrodes. They injected him with a radiopaque liquid and watched it go up and down in X rays as they tilted his bed. After two weeks, he left the hospital. The doctors told Hawking only that his was an unusual case and that he did not have multiple sclerosis, a degenerative disease of the central nervous system. Depressed, he returned to Cambridge to await the results of the test and assumed that matters would only get worse. It was not long until he heard that the doctors had diagnosed him as having amyotrophic lateral sclerosis (ALS), which in Britain is commonly known as motor neuron disease and in the United States as Lou Gehrig's disease.

The doctors estimated that Hawking had only two years to live. Although they had no real idea of whether he would live only a few months or many years, they assumed that he would die quickly because he had developed ALS at a much younger age than most people who get the disease. They told Hawking that the disease was unpredictable, that it would stop progressing for periods of time, that patients would get no better during these periods but they would simply get no worse. Then most patients would go into another period of swift decline before leveling off again. The normal course of ALS is that it causes the muscles to atrophy, leading to immobility and then paralysis. Gradually, speech becomes more difficult and eventually impossible. The patient has difficulty swallowing. Death occurs when the respiratory muscles are affected and the patient contracts pneumonia or suffocates. Throughout it all, the functions of the mind, including memory, remain unaffected. Although the disease is entirely painless, patients in the later stages of ALS are often given morphine to ease depression.

The diagnosis understandably threw Hawking into a deep depression. His doctors advised him to continue his research at Cambridge. But to Hawking, that seemed utterly pointless, just a senseless way of keeping his mind occupied while he was dying. For a while, he retreated to his rooms at Cambridge and listened to music, becoming what he later called a "tragic character." Although Hawking continued to wonder why the disease happened to him, he never let himself fall completely into self-pity. He remembered a young boy who had been in the adjacent bed while he was in the hospital undergoing his tests. The boy died of leukemia. "It had not been a pretty sight," recalled Hawking, "Clearly there were people who were worse off than me. At least my condition didn't make me feel sick. Whenever I feel inclined to be sorry for myself, I remember that boy."

Meanwhile, Hawking's father was doing everything he could to learn more about ALS and possible therapies. He discussed similar illnesses with many of his colleagues in the field of tropical medicine. He even called American virologist Daniel Carleton Gajdusek, who had won the 1976 Nobel Prize in medicine for his work on a comparable illness in Borneo. But it was all to no avail. All of the doctors said that there was nothing that could be done, no physical therapy or medication that could slow the progress of the disease. Dr. Hawking then decided to intervene with Dennis Sciama on his son's behalf. Because his son was not expected to live the three years that was the minimum length of time for doctoral studies, he asked Sciama if it was possible for his son to complete his Ph.D. work in a shorter period of time. Sciama said that he could not bend the rules. He knew what Stephen Hawking was capable of and he was unwilling to let him compromise.

While Hawking was in the hospital, he began to have strange dreams. In one, he dreamt that he was going to be executed. In another, a recurring dream, he dreamt that he would sacrifice his life to save others. He realized that there were many valuable contributions that he could make if his life was spared. He had the incredible good fortune to be in one of the few fields where he could do most of his work in his head. If he had been an experimental physicist rather than a theoretical physicist, his career would probably have been over. Before his illness, Hawking had been rather bored with life, but now he realized that life was indeed worthwhile. Besides, his relationship with Jane Wilde was progressing, and she was helping him emerge from his depression. Hawking returned to his studies, determined that, if he was going to die, he might as well do some good while he was still able to. For the first time in his life, he was going to commit himself to his work.

In January 1931, physicist Albert Einstein jots down an equation relating to the generalized theory of gravitation during a lecture in Pasadena, California. The equations Einstein developed for the theory of general relativity predicted that the universe had to be either expanding or contracting, and they led to a new era in cosmological research.

4

EARLY
BREAKTHROUGHS

ALTHOUGH HAWKING WAS NOW EAGER to make progress on his research, he continued to flounder for another year. His main obstacle was the lack of an appropriate research problem, one that would be sufficiently complicated to satisfy the requirements for a Ph.D. In 1961, Dennis Sciama organized a group of graduate students at Cambridge University to study relativity and cosmology. At the time, he was the only person in England teaching relativity. As the 1960s progressed, new developments in astronomy gave rise to an explosion of interest in these subjects. But when Hawking entered Cambridge and became part of Sciama's relativity group, it was still such a new field that there were not a lot of easily identifiable dissertation topics available. Although Sciama tried to suggest directions of research to students, often they would just stumble across a problem, and Sciama would tell them to go ahead with it.

Albert Einstein had published his ground-breaking paper on his theory of general relativity in 1916. Essentially, it was a theory of gravity's effect on space-time. Einstein predicted that the light from distant stars would bend as it passed by the sun because it was moving through space-time that was warped by the sun's mass. As the light changed direction, it would alter the apparent position of the stars in the sky. It was surmised that during a total eclipse of the sun, in which the sun's light is completely blocked, the bending of the light could be observed because the apparent position of the stars near the sun would shift. In 1919, a total eclipse of the sun occurred and photographs were taken showing that the shift was real and that Einstein's theory was correct.

The equations that Einstein had developed for the theory of general relativity also predicted that the universe had to be either expanding or contracting, that it could not be static. This was contrary to what everyone, including Einstein himself, believed at the time. Einstein spent the next few years trying to change the equations so that they would predict a static universe. By the early 1930s, however, powerful new telescopes had been built through which observations were made that confirmed that the universe was expanding. Einstein had to admit that his original equations had been accurate, and he called his efforts to change the equations "the greatest blunder of my life."

By the 1960s there were two basic schools of thought about the origins and operation of the universe that incorporated the observation that the universe was expanding. The first was the steady state theory. This theory claimed that, as the universe expanded and galaxies moved farther apart from one another, matter would form from nothing in the empty space and eventually consolidate into new galaxies. Because these new galaxies were always replacing old, dying ones, the universe would always look about the same.

The second view was the big bang theory of the origin of the universe. Proponents of this view derided the steady-staters' proposal that matter could be created in space out of nothing. They argued instead that if the universe is expanding, then in the past all of the matter in it must have been closer together. If one went far enough into the past, they speculated, then all of the matter in the universe must have been in one infinitely dense point that exploded, forming all of the particles and gases that would eventually combine to create galaxies. Although in the 1940s and 1950s this theory was regarded as preposterous, by the 1960s, astronomers were making many observations that lent it credence. Big bang theorists had predicted that the universe was filled with cold background radiation left over from the initial explosion. In 1965, radio astronomers detected background microwave radiation throughout space, exactly as had been predicted.

This discovery convinced Dennis Sciama and many other scientists who had previously adhered to the steady state model that the big bang theory was correct. But it did not convince Fred Hoyle, who had been one of the developers of the steady state model and remained one of its most dogged defenders. Hoyle had, in fact, coined the term "big bang" as a way of denigrating the opposing theory. Much to Hoyle's amusement, it quickly moved into common usage, although without being considered derisive. For Hoyle, the theory of the big bang was just not dignified; he once likened it to a woman jumping out of a birthday cake.

Fred Hoyle was the star physicist at Cambridge when Hawking arrived in 1962. Although Hoyle was not assigned to be Hawking's supervisor, he did advise a few other graduate students. Jayant Narlikar, one of his students, happened to occupy an office adjacent to Hawking's. As part of his course of study, he was doing some of the mathematics for Hoyle's research on the origin of the universe. In the collegial atmosphere of the physics department, students often shared their research with one another in order to get suggestions or stimulate ideas for new approaches. Hawking became very interested in what Narlikar was working on, and the two soon began exchanging pages of equations. Because Hawking had still not found a research problem for himself and Narlikar's work fascinated him, he spent considerable time studying Narlikar's research and developing it further.

After a few months, Hoyle decided to announce his latest findings in a public forum—a meeting of the Royal Society in London. Following his lecture, he asked if there were any questions. Because Hawking had been so interested in Hoyle's research, he was, of course, in attendance. In front of the audience of distinguished scientists, Hawking rose to speak. "The quantity you're talking about diverges," he stated. A wave of murmurs ran through the crowd. The audience knew that if Hawking's statement was correct, then Hoyle's latest findings were completely wrong.

Hoyle responded, "Of course it doesn't diverge."

The room was completely silent. Hawking was insistent. "It does," he asserted.

Hoyle's anger was growing. "How do you know?" he growled.

"Because I worked it out," Hawking replied.

The audience laughed nervously. Hoyle was furious with Hawking and claimed that his actions were unprofessional and unethical. Hawking, in turn, accused Hoyle of being unethical for announcing results that had not been verified. In this case, Hawking's research was correct. Hoyle had been hasty in announcing his findings. Hawking then wrote a paper explaining his conclusions, and it was well received by his colleagues. Although he was still only a graduate student, Hawking had already established himself as an important figure in the field of cosmology.

While Hawking's scientific career was advancing, his relationship with Jane Wilde had grown and the two had fallen in love. They became engaged, and Wilde, who was now studying in London, made more frequent visits to Cambridge on the weekends. She had never known Hawking when he was completely healthy, so his increasing disability did not bother her. She recalled, "I wanted to find some purpose to my existence, and I suppose I found it in the idea of looking after him. But we were in love." In turn, Hawking said that Wilde gave him "the will to live." Their engagement also spurred him on to complete his thesis. If they were to get married, he had to get a job, and to do that, he had to complete his degree.

Luckily, at about this time a good research problem for Hawking's thesis finally emerged. Dennis Sciama had begun taking his relativity students to London to converse with a young mathematician named Roger Penrose. Penrose, who had been a student of Sciama's in the 1950s, was one of the most brilliant mathematicians ever to work in cosmology. In the early 1960s, he was studying singularities, points in space-time of infinite density. Although general relativity posited their existence, no one really believed that they were physical realities. Penrose, however, applied new mathematical methods to prove that when a star collapsed beyond a certain point, it had to end up as a singularity. Previously, people had believed that a star would have to be perfectly symmetrical for this to happen. Otherwise, they thought, it would be possible for the collapsing matter to pass itself in space and not all be condensed into a single point.

Penrose's results sparked an idea in Hawking's mind. It occurred to him that he could adapt Penrose's singularity theory to the whole universe. By imagining the expanding universe as the reverse of a collapsing star, the same considerations would apply at the beginning of time. At some point in the past, Hawking thought, perhaps all of the matter in the universe was contained in one singularity.

He proposed this question as a dissertation topic to Sciama who told him to go ahead with it. Finally, he had an appropriately rigorous topic for his thesis.

Over the next few months Hawking delved into the problem, working hard for the first time in his life. Sciama soon realized that Hawking was doing something truly remarkable. Singularities involve infinite quantities that

Roger Penrose, who had been a student of Dennis Sciama's during the 1950s, was one of the brightest mathematicians ever to work in cosmology. After reading Penrose's theorem that any body undergoing gravitational collapse must ultimately form a singularity, Hawking used it to prove there should be a singularity only if the universe was expanding fast enough to avoid collapsing again. In 1970, Hawking and Penrose published a joint paper that proved there must have been a big bang singularity with the understanding that general relativity is correct.

the laws of physics, including general relativity, cannot accommodate, so these laws would not apply. If the universe began in a singularity, it "would not just be an interesting result," explained Dennis Sciama, "it would create an intellectual crisis because it would mean that general relativity breaks down at the very beginning of the universe." Because scientists could not apply any physical laws to a singularity, it would be impossible to predict what happened before them or what would emerge from them. Sciama said of Hawking's research on the subject, "It was a brilliant piece of work."

The last chapter of Hawking's dissertation contained what was in fact his first singularity theorem for the origin of the universe. "There is a singularity in our past," he wrote in his thesis. Before he would be awarded his degree, his thesis had to be approved by a group of examiners. Although the early chapters were somewhat chaotic because of his intellectual floundering during his first two years at Cambridge, the examiners agreed that the last chapter, which dealt with the singularity theory for the beginning of the universe, was brilliant. At age 23, he was now Dr. Stephen W. Hawking.

After the award of Hawking's doctorate, Hawking and Penrose were off and running. They spent the next few years studying black holes, singularities, and their properties. They became known as the two great relativists working in cosmology. Penrose had already proposed the theory that all singularities must be hidden inside a black hole, so if the laws of physics did break down at a singularity, there would still be no way for an observer to see what was happening. With Hawking, however, he worked out a proof that, if general relativity was correct, then there must have been a singularity at the beginning of the universe. This was the one singularity, the two physicists explained, that was not hidden inside a black hole. They also established that black holes could rotate, and Penrose showed that a rotating black hole could lose energy.

These three photographs illustrate a two-dimensional model of a three-dimensional universe. The resulting expanding universe is a two-dimensional sphere like the surface of a balloon being blown up. Objects that exist in this universe can only move along the surface; in other words, they cannot exist inside or outside the balloon. The white dots on the surface represent typical points in the universe. All points on the surface expand away from all other points—the more the balloon is blown up, the farther the points move away from each other. No one point can be considered as the center of the universe or the point from which the big bang began. The three images shown here depict only the early behavior of an expanding universe. The universe starts out very hot (top) and eventually cools (bottom).

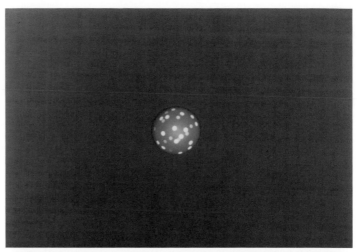

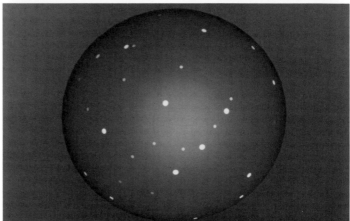

Hawking also proposed the existence of miniholes, black holes that were smaller than the nucleus of an atom. He suggested that the miniholes had been created at the time of the big bang and that they still exist. Immediately after the big bang, densities were much higher than they are now. Hawking theorized that portions of the newly expanding universe that were slightly denser than the rest would get pinched off and form these primordial mini-holes. His pioneering ideas and discoveries established Hawking as one of the world's preeminent authorities on black holes.

In June 1965, Stephen Hawking married Jane Wilde. Although they both realized that Hawking might die at any moment, they were determined to make the best of their situation and live as normal a life as possible. Their most immediate problem was finding housing. After Hawking received his doctoral degree, he was awarded a fellowship to Caius College at Cambridge. Fellowships are paid positions of which the primary obligation of the recipients is merely to continue their research. By this time Hawking could walk only with the aid of canes, so it was imperative that the Hawkings find housing in the middle of Cambridge, within a very short distance of the Department of Applied Mathematics and Theoretical Physics (DAMTP) where Hawking would be doing his work. Even though the Hawkings had special needs, the college made no exception to its policy of not assisting fellows in finding housing. Luckily, the couple soon heard about a small house that was available less than 100 yards away from the DAMTP and gladly rented it. A few months later they moved into another house just down the street, where they would remain for many years. Jane Hawking still had one more year of study before she could receive her degree, however, so in 1965 she continued her trips between London and Cambridge on the weekends.

When she finally moved full time to Cambridge in 1966, the Hawkings became the center of social activity within

The Department of Applied Mathematics and Theoretical Physics (DAMTP) is located on Silver Street in Cambridge. After Hawking received his Ph.D. in 1965, he was given a fellowship by Caius College at Cambridge and did his research at the DAMPT. By this time, Hawking had married Jane Wilde and was having great difficulty walking.

the physics community. Jane Hawking made sure that they were as active as any young couple. Their house was a cheerful place, the site of innumerable dinner parties replete with animated discussions shouted over blaring classical music. In 1967, their first child, Robert, was born. A daughter, Lucy, was born in 1970 and another son, Timothy, followed in 1979.

Jane Hawking probably knew what she had given up by marrying a severely disabled man. She would never be able to focus entirely on her career the way her husband was destined to on his. It was all she could do to care for her husband and three children because Hawking was unable to help with housework or childcare. Jane Hawking found herself frustrated in those early years of marriage. She was left with the drudgery of everyday life while Hawking was accumulating prizes, academic honors, and other accolades.

Caring for Hawking was also becoming more arduous. Although the progress of his disease had slowed after its initial onset, during the late 1960s his body began to deteriorate rapidly. He was unable to get around without the use of crutches and his speech was beginning to become slurred. He remained adamantly independent, however, refusing to let anyone help him. Roger Penrose remembers being at the Hawking home and watching him struggle for 15 minutes to get up the winding staircase to his bedroom. Hawking declined all offers of assistance, not only out of obstinacy but because pulling himself up the stairs was considered a rudimentary form of physical therapy. His condition continued to decline, however, and in 1970 he was forced to begin using a wheelchair. Nothing could stop the upward arc of his career, though. In the next few years, he was destined for scientific glory.

In 1989, Hawking and his wife, Jane, attend a ceremony at Cambridge, where Hawking received an honorary award. Hawking's research on black holes brought him world renown and revolutionized the way scientists view the universe.

5

BLACK HOLES
AND BEYOND

WHEN HAWKING WAS STILL in graduate school, he and his fellow student George Ellis had drawn up a list of projects for themselves for the future. One item on the list was that they each planned to get married. Another was that they intended to write a book together on cosmology. Although they were both very busy, by the late 1960s they found time to start work on the manuscript. They decided that the book would be a treatise on classical cosmology, which, in its original form, contained very little of Hawking's recent research.

After Hawking and Ellis divided up the topics to be covered in the book, it took them six years to write the manuscript. By the time they had begun work on the book, Hawking could no longer write, and therefore had to dictate all of his material to Ellis. They found a publisher, Cambridge University Press, which was eager to produce their book because it was just initiating a series of academic texts aimed at professional physicists. Hawking and Ellis's volume, *The Large-Scale Structure of Spacetime*, was an ideal candidate for inclusion in the series. Finally published in 1973, Hawking and Ellis's book was very well received and is today considered a classic in the field.

The book was unusually complicated, filled with equations that made it unintelligible to anyone except experts in the field. Even many professionals found it incomprehensible. Shortly after its publication, Hawking encountered John Shakeshaft, a radio astronomer, on a train returning from the Royal Astronomical Society in London. Shakeshaft told Hawking that he had bought a copy of his book. When Hawking asked how he liked it, Shakeshaft replied, "Well, I thought I might make it to page 10, but I only got as far as page 4, and I've given up, I'm afraid." Having sold 3,500 copies in hardback and 13,000 in paperback, it is one of the best-selling research books ever published by Cambridge University Press. Many of the copies were sold years later, however, after Hawking's reputation had moved beyond the small circle of theoretical physicists.

Meanwhile, Hawking and Penrose continued to study black holes. When Hawking had first thought of applying the concept of entropy to black holes, he was using it only as an analogy. What would happen, he had wondered, if two black holes collided? He realized that no matter how the holes merged or transformed each other, the surface area of the event horizon would have to increase or perhaps stay the same size. Under no conditions could it decrease. It occurred to him that this notion was similar to the rule in thermodynamics that says that the entropy of a closed system can only increase, never decrease. After discussing the idea with Penrose, Hawking decided that the relationship between entropy and black holes was merely an interesting coincidence and a convenient analogy. By 1972, Hawking was also working with a colleague from graduate school, Brandon Carter, and an American researcher, James Bardeen. The three physicists found more connections between entropy and black holes, but they continued to consider them only analogies, useful for mathematical shortcuts.

A young graduate student named Jacob Bekenstein, however, was taking the connections much more seriously. He was a student at Princeton University in New Jersey, working under John Wheeler, the man who had coined the term "black hole." Bekenstein decided to apply thermodynamics directly to the study of black holes. Using elaborate mathematical calculations, he suggested in his Ph.D. thesis that the area of the event horizon of a black hole might literally be the measure of the entropy of a black hole. Bekenstein was claiming that the properties of thermodynamics were really at work.

Hawking, Carter, and Bardeen were incensed by the young researcher's proposition. According to Hawking, the main problem with Bekenstein's conclusions was that if black holes literally had an entropy then they also had to have a temperature. But everyone knew that black holes had a temperature of absolute zero, because nothing, not even the radiation necessary for heat, could escape from them. After Bekenstein published his findings in a paper entitled "Black Hole Thermodynamics," the three older men shot back with an article called "The Four Laws of Black Hole Mechanics." By pointedly omitting the term "thermodynamics," they were emphasizing that it could not possibly be applicable because it required radiation.

Hawking was still feuding with Bekenstein in 1973 when he decided to visit the Soviet researcher Yakov Zeldovich in Moscow. While there, he met with Zeldovich's colleague, Alex Starobinsky, who suggested that rotating black holes might throw off particles. Roger Penrose had already shown that it was possible to derive energy from a rotating black hole, just as it was from any other spinning object. Although Hawking was not completely convinced by Starobinsky's conclusions, he did

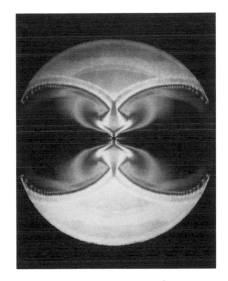

A supercomputer-generated simulation shows an accretion disk surrounding a black hole (center). The accretion disk is a swirling accumulation of gas, dust, and other matter, much of which will be sucked into the black hole. Although no real black hole has yet been conclusively located, there are now several possible contenders under observation, including Cygnus X-1.

The spiral galaxy NGC (New General Catalog)–4565 is a member of the Local Supercluster, a conglomerate of thousands of galaxies. The bright, central spherical shape is crammed with stars and conceals at its nucleus some as-yet-unknown energy source—perhaps a gigantic black hole. During the early 1970s, Hawking's research on black holes, especially his paper on black hole radiation, became the first step in the uni-fication of quantum mechanics and general relativity.

not scoff at them. Because he did not like the way in which Starobinsky had arrived at his conclusions, upon his return to Cambridge, Hawking decided to redo the calculations himself.

As with all of the problems on which theoretical physicists work, the calculations necessary to determine particle emission of rotating black holes are incredibly complex. Hawking decided that before he tried to replicate Starobinsky's results, he would first try to determine the rate of emission for a black hole that was not rotating. Because he knew that the result should be that there was no particle emission, he could be sure that he had the equations set up properly. After two months of arranging the equations in his head, he finally worked them out and was very annoyed to find that they showed that stationary black holes should be emitting an infinite number of particles.

Hawking was convinced that he must have simply made a mistake in the calculations. He spent the next month doing the mathematics over and over again, but he kept getting the same result. He was hesitant to tell anyone what he had discovered because he did not want Jacob Bekenstein to find out about it. This was just the sort of result that Bekenstein needed as ammunition in his argument that thermodynamics worked on black holes—an argument that Hawking was still not willing to accept. He later admitted that he "put quite a lot of effort into trying to get rid of this embarrassing effect" simply out of irritation with Bekenstein and his theories. Finally, he was forced to believe his own calculations rather than his usually infallible intuition.

Only then did Hawking incorporate the notion of virtual particles from quantum mechanics into his theory in order to account for black hole radiation. This completely altered

Hawking gives a lecture at Northeastern University in Boston in 1990. Hawking once wrote that detecting a black hole "might seem a bit like looking for a black cat in a coal cellar." However, black holes are not really black, he continued, "they glow like a hot body, the smaller they are, the more they glow."

physicists' understanding of black holes and contradicted many of Hawking's own earlier beliefs. He now realized that it was possible for the surface area of a black hole to shrink. Not only that, but if the black hole did not have new material coming into it, then when Hawking radiation was taken into account, black holes must shrink. For the majority of black holes, those that were the result of a dead star, Hawking radiation would never be noticeable. The black hole would always swallow up enough mass from the adjacent space to counteract the effect of its loss of mass due to Hawking radiation.

Hawking radiation could have a profound effect, however, on the miniholes that Hawking had already determined should exist. Because of the small size of these miniholes, they would not be able to absorb enough mass from around them to compensate for Hawking radiation. The radiation gives the black hole a temperature that is inversely related to the mass of the hole. The smaller a black hole gets, the hotter it gets. Hawking realized that eventually the radiation would make the mini black hole so hot that it would explode. The publication of Hawking's theory instigated a search for exploding black holes.

Astronomers had already been looking for regular black holes and in the early 1970s had discovered what they thought was an excellent prospect. Black holes are detectable only because astronomers can see the result of their gravitational pull. Astronomers had been looking for them in binary systems, pairs of stars that rotate around one another, because then the black hole would be rotating around a normal, visible star. Binary star systems are easily identifiable because the pull of gravity of the two stars on each other affects their movement. Astronomers can estimate the mass of the visible star and the unseen object based upon the way that they move in their orbits. Any dead star with a mass of at least three times that of the sun collapses in on itself and becomes a black hole. So if the unseen object had at least three solar masses, it should

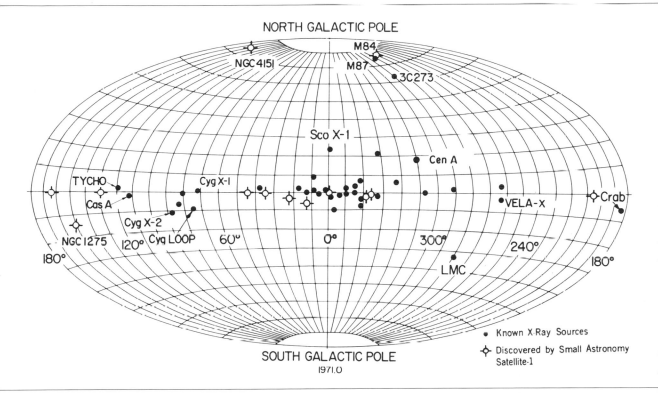

NORTH GALACTIC POLE

M84
NGC 4151   M87
3C 273

Sco X-1

Cen A

TYCHO   Cyg X-1
Cas A   Crab
Cyg X-2   VELA-X
NGC 1275   120° Cyg LOOP   60°   0°   300°   240°   180°
180°   LMC

SOUTH GALACTIC POLE
1971.0

• Known X-Ray Sources
⟡ Discovered by Small Astronomy Satellite-1

be a black hole. During the early 1970s, astronomers noticed Cygnus X-1, a binary system in which one of the objects has a mass of 8 to 10 times that of the sun. Scientists believe that this is the most likely contender for being a black hole.

Still, there was no conclusive evidence that Cygnus X-1 was a black hole or even that black holes existed at all. In 1975, Hawking made a bet with his friend Kip Thorne, a professor of theoretical physics at the California Institute of Technology. If Cygnus X-1 turned out to be a black hole, Thorne would get a one-year subscription to *Penthouse* magazine. If it was not a black hole, Hawking would receive a four-year subscription to the British satirical magazine *Private Eye*. Hawking joked that the bet was an insurance policy. If it turned out that black holes do not exist, his life's work would be wasted, but at least he would

Cygnus X-1 is thought to consist of a black hole and a normal star. According to Hawking, "The number of black holes . . . in the long history of the universe . . . may well be greater even than the number of visible stars, which totals about a hundred thousand million in our galaxy alone."

The Hawkings moved to this home on 5 West Road in Cambridge during the mid-1970s. As Hawking's fame grew, his physical condition worsened and he required a full-time personal assistant. Although the assistant was also expected to perform various domestic tasks, the position became a highly prized one for it provided students with valuable time to learn from their mentor.

have the consolation of the magazine subscription. If they did exist, he would gladly lose the bet. It would not be until 1990, after a period of 20 years during which astronomers had not come up with a reasonable alternative explanation for Cygnus X-1, that Hawking would finally admit that it was a black hole and that he had lost the bet.

Black holes entered the mainstream of public consciousness in the early 1970s. Because of Hawking's many contributions to understanding black holes, he began to be in demand by the media. Hawking was mentioned in newspaper articles, and he appeared in television documentaries on black holes. Soon, Hawking became the star of these shows. In 1977, the BBC broadcast *The Key to the Universe*, a program that not only discussed Hawking's achievements and attempts at unifying relativity and quantum mechanics, but also covered his personal life and his disability. He was becoming not just the man who knew about black holes but a celebrity in and of himself.

During this same period, the scientific community was also recognizing Hawking's achievements. In March 1974, after he stunned the world with his findings about Hawking radiation, he was invited to become a Fellow of the Royal Society, Britain's highest academic honor. He was only 32 years old at the time, one of the youngest scientists ever to become a Royal Society Fellow. Other prizes and accolades soon followed. He received the Pius XII Medal from the Pontifical Academy of Science at the Vatican, the Eddington Medal from the Royal Astronomical Society, and the Hughes Medal from the Royal Society, as well as the Hopkins, Dannie Heinemann, and Maxwell prizes, all for his remarkable achievements in the study of black holes. In 1978, he received the Albert Einstein Award, one of the most prestigious prizes in physics, for his work toward a unified theory.

Cambridge University was slower to recognize the man who was becoming its favorite son. In 1975, he was promoted to the position of reader in Gravitational Physics, a position above a fellow, but not yet a professor. By the time of his television fame in 1977, there were complaints in the academic community that Cambridge's most illustrious scientist had not yet been given a professorship. In March 1977, the university finally offered Hawking the chair of Gravitational Physics, a position created specifically for him.

Because of Hawking's physical condition, he has fewer responsibilities than most teachers at Cambridge. He is not required to teach courses or spend large amounts of time on administrative duties, and as a result, he has more of an opportunity to do research or to ponder physics. He does oversee the relativity group and advises a small number of students. These students tend to agree that he is an excellent teacher because he is willing to spend more time with them than most professors. While other professors are often distant, Hawking can frequently be found in the break room, drinking coffee and discussing whatever projects the students are currently working on.

As Hawking's fame grew, his physical condition worsened. By the mid-1970s, he was unable to feed himself or to get in and out of bed without help. Until this time, Jane Hawking had functioned as her husband's full-time nurse, but she could no longer handle the task by herself. At about the same time, the Hawkings moved into a larger, one-floor apartment. The new flat had wide doorways and large rooms, which enabled Hawking to maneuver his wheelchair throughout the whole apartment. Because there was now extra space, they decided to have one of Hawking's research assistants move in with them, and in exchange for free room and board, the student helped care for Hawking. Over the years, a number of graduate students filled this position as Hawking's personal assistant. Although the assistant was expected to babysit the children, help out around the house, and perform secretarial duties, it became a prized position for most research assistants. Inevitably, they became very close to Hawking, and he would serve as an important reference for them in the future. The arrangement worked out well for all concerned, relieving Jane's burden, giving Stephen the help he needed, and providing the assistants with the valuable opportunity to learn from him.

Hawking's mobility also improved in the mid 1970s when he began traveling in an electric wheelchair. Previously, when he had to go any distance he drove a three-wheeled car. Whenever he used the car, however, he always had to make sure that someone would meet him at his destination to help him get out of the car and into his wheelchair. When he used the electric wheelchair, he became more independent because he could go places on the spur of the moment. For example, he simply had to leave the house and put the wheelchair into high gear—he could travel quite quickly. He enjoyed making people who were accompanying him run alongside him. The electric wheelchair also allowed Hawking to whiz around the yard when he played tag with his children.

As Hawking's speech became less intelligible and his facial expressions more difficult to control, he began using the wheelchair as a way of expressing himself. When he was angry or annoyed, he aimed for the feet of the object of his ire. Remembering Hawking's liberal political leanings, a former student noted that one of Hawking's great regrets is that he never had the chance to run over the toes of Margaret Thatcher, the conservative former prime minister of Great Britain. With the freedom that the motorized chair gave him, Hawking's future seemed limitless.

Hawking poses with his family. From left to right are his daughter, Lucy, his two sons, Robert and Timothy, and his wife, Jane. When Hawking began to use an electric wheelchair he became more independent because he could go places on the spur of the moment. It also enabled him to play tag with his children in the backyard.

Hawking sits in front of a painting of Sir Isaac Newton. In 1979, Cambridge honored Hawking with the post of Lucasian Professor of Mathematics, the position Newton himself had been given in 1669.

6

TO KNOW THE
MIND OF GOD

IN 1979, CAMBRIDGE UNIVERSITY selected Hawking to be the Lucasian Professor of Mathematics. Because the history of science is very important to Hawking, he considered this post to be among the highest possible honors. More than 300 years before, in 1669, Isaac Newton had been appointed to the same position. Earning a professorship at Cambridge was an uncommon achievement in itself, and Hawking had done it at the relatively young age of 37.

At Cambridge, there is a book that all professors are supposed to sign at the time of their appointment. Not until a year after Hawking's promotion to the Lucasian Chair did university officials realize that his signature did not yet appear in the book. They brought the book to his office and he slowly, exactingly, signed his name. He did not know it then, but it was the last time he was able to sign his name.

At the ceremony commemorating his appointment to the Lucasian Chair, Hawking gave a lecture entitled "Is the End in Sight for Theoretical Physics?" In his speech, he suggested that the Grand Unification Theory might be determined by the end of the century. Scientists were making new discoveries at such a rapid rate that he felt it might be possible to uncover the fundamental laws governing both general relativity and quantum mechanics within the next 20 years. To achieve this, Hawking explained, physicists would have to reconcile the four fundamental forces of physics—gravity, electromagnetism, the strong nuclear force that works on the level of the atom, and the weak nuclear force that governs radioactive decay. Although finding the unified theory might mean the end of theoretical physics, in that physicists would have achieved a fundamental understanding of the laws of the universe, it would not put Hawking out of a job. "There would still be lots to do," he later said, "but it would be like mountaineering after Everest."

Discovering a unified theory would, in all probability, help physicists understand the conditions at the beginning of the universe. If scientists succeeded in formulating a Theory of Everything, Hawking wrote in his 1988 book, *A Brief History of Time: From the Big Bang to Black Holes,* "Then we shall all, philosophers, scientists and just ordinary people, be able to take part in the discussion of the question of why it is that we and the universe exist. If we can find the answer to that, it would be the ultimate triumph of human reason—for then we would know the mind of God."

In 1980, although Hawking was still known primarily for his work on black holes, the connections he had already made between quantum mechanics and general relativity in his discovery of black hole radiation made him one of the major aspirants for discovering the Theory of Everything. More and more, Hawking focused his attention on

considering the origin of the universe and finding a unified theory.

At a conference on cosmology at the Vatican in 1981,
Hawking announced some of his newest ideas about the
origin of the universe. The purpose of the conference was
to discuss the development of the universe following the
big bang. Throughout history, the Catholic church had
been opposed to scientists delving into the origin of the
universe. By the time of the 1981 conference, however, the
Catholic church believed that it was acceptable to theorize
about the nature of the universe. But during Pope John
Paul II's address to the conference, the pope suggested that
scientists should leave the question of the actual beginning
of the universe to religion. He said the question of why the
universe began and what happened at the very moment of
creation should be answered by metaphysicians rather than
physicists. (Metaphysics is the division of philosophy that
investigates the fundamental nature of reality and being.)

After Pope John Paul II's speech, the attendees of the
conference had the opportunity to be introduced to him
individually. Each physicist took turns walking onto the
stage where the pope was sitting, kneeling before him,
speaking to him for a few moments, and then exiting the
stage. When Hawking rolled onto the stage, however, it
was the pope who knelt. In order to see Hawking at eye
level, Pope John Paul II had to kneel beside his wheelchair.
The pope spoke to Hawking longer than he had talked to
any of the other physicists, though this might have been
because of Hawking's difficulty in speaking. When their
conversation ended, the pope rose, dusted himself off,
smiled at Hawking, and returned to his chair. Some on-
lookers believed that Pope John Paul II had shown Hawking more respect than he deserved. Hawking's reputation
as a man who thinks that religion is irrelevant in understanding the universe had been growing more pronounced.
Others wondered if the pope understood the implications

After Pope John Paul II addressed the cosmology conference at the Vatican in 1981, he was introduced to the gathered scientists individually. When he met Hawking, the pope kneeled before him in order to speak to him at eye level, and they conversed. At the conference Hawking had proposed that there was a new way to view the universe, one that did not need a creator.

of the lecture Hawking had given two days earlier, in which he had proposed a new way of viewing the universe, one that removed the need for a creator entirely.

Audaciously, Hawking had chosen the Vatican conference as the place to unveil his new theory—the no boundary model of the universe. Hawking suggested in this new theory that there was no beginning to space-time. One way of looking at the evolving and expanding universe is to picture it as a balloon that is being inflated. The surface of the balloon represents both space and time, and consequently, as the balloon is blown up, both space and time expand. Many physicists believed by this time that the universe would eventually stop expanding and collapse back in on itself, a concept that is commonly called the big crunch.

Hawking suggested that if, instead of using an expanding balloon as a model for the universe, one substitutes the earth, then it is possible to consider the history of the universe as a whole. From the north pole to the equator, the earth expands. From the latitude of the equator, it shrinks back down to being merely a point again at the south pole. Although the north and south poles are points, which in this model represent the big bang and the big crunch, there are no edges. Thus, there is no beginning or end to time. At the north pole, the only possible direction to go is south. Analogously, at the moment of the big bang, there is only the future; there is no past. In this sense, there is no way to conceive of a "before." The universe has no boundaries, no beginning.

At the Vatican conference, Hawking's arguments were still couched in complicated mathematical terms. Although he had not yet articulated what they might mean for religion, he later wrote about their religious implications in his book *A Brief History of Time*. "So long as the universe had a beginning, we could suppose it had a creator. But if the universe is really completely self-contained, having no boundary or edge, it would have neither beginning nor end: it would simply be. What place, then, for a creator?"

The no boundary theory also bypassed one of the difficulties in the effort to marry quantum mechanics and general relativity. In classical cosmology, general relativity always broke down at the singularity at the beginning of time. In Hawking's new theory, however, the mathematics of general relativity never broke down because there was no beginning.

To develop the no boundary proposal, Hawking used geometric rather than mathematical models. This is typical of the way he works. Because he has to do all of the math in his head, Hawking finds complicated equations with many variables daunting and therefore avoids the sorts of questions that require complicated mathematics. Even before the onset of ALS, Hawking was more adept at geometrical than mathematical ways of thinking, so he thought in terms that he could visualize, such as graphs and geometrical concepts, rather than in equations. His ability to imagine four-dimensional geometry is uncommon, even within the community of theoretical physicists.

As his body deteriorated, Hawking used his unique abilities in increasingly brash ways. By 1980, he told his friend, Kip Thorne, "I'd rather be right than rigorous." Rigor, or exactitude, is essential in the realm of mathematics. During the 1960s and 1970s, Hawking, like mathematicians, had sought absolute proof for his theories. By the time of the Vatican conference, he had become impatient in his quest for the unification theory. He had always made his discoveries by taking intuitive leaps and then figuring out a method by which to demonstrate that his intuition was correct. He was seeking a higher truth, a complete understanding of the laws of the universe. Rather than waiting until he was mathematically sure that a theory was correct, if there was a high probability that it was correct, he would accept it and build on it. Because he was becoming increasingly disabled and death was always within sight, he could not afford to waste any time in his quest to understand the nature of the universe.

Meanwhile, Cambridge University Press was preparing to publish another book by Hawking. In 1979, he had edited *General Relativity: An Einstein Centenary Survey,* which had been published in commemoration of the 100th anniversary of Einstein's birth. The book had sold very well, primarily because of Hawking's association with it; thus Cambridge University Press was pleased with his increasing fame. But as Hawking grew more famous, he also became more demanding, and when his subsequent book, *Superspace and Supergravity,* was set to go to press, a confrontation arose. This volume was part of the same series of books as his first text, and it was expected to sell roughly the same number of copies. Hawking wanted a certain photograph of the blackboard in his office to be used on the cover of the book. The cartoons and doodlings in the picture were in color and would have to be reproduced in color if they were to be at all comprehensible. The Cambridge editors knew that such a complex research book would never sell enough copies to justify the expense of a color cover. Hawking was obstinate, however, and threatened to withdraw the book from publication if the publisher did not agree to his demands. Cambridge University Press finally agreed, but the editors' prediction eventually proved right: the book did not sell enough copies to recoup the cost of the color cover.

Hawking's fame became useful to him in other disagreements in which he was involved. For years, he had

In 1979, Hawking receives the Man of the Year award from the Royal Association for Disability and Rehabilitation. Hawking became a vocal disabled rights advocate and fought with city officials to have lower curbs constructed along the roads in Cambridge to make public places accessible to the physically impaired.

The Hawkings and a private nurse make their way to an award ceremony in Cambridge. Although the monetary awards Hawking received for his work permitted him to hire private nurses to help care for him, the financial strain of his illness and the educational needs of his children became oppressive.

been clashing with Cambridge University over wheelchair access to buildings. Only a few years earlier, it had required a long and bitter argument with university officials to persuade them to pay for a ramp to be installed for easy admittance to the DAMTP building. Hawking had also persuaded them to lower the curbs along the roads between his home and the DAMTP building. Emboldened by his success, he began to fight with the city of Cambridge for rights for other disabled people. Hawking had been particularly incensed when a building that was used as a polling place was not accessible to the disabled. City officials argued that the building was not actually a public building, and thus was not subject to the Disabled Person's Act, which legislated access requirements. Because of Hawking's celebrity, the press became interested in the dispute. Eventually, after receiving much public pressure about the situation, the city agreed to improve access to the building.

Although Hawking loathed being thought of as a disabled scientist—he preferred to be considered a scientist who happened to have a disability—he became increasingly vocal as a disabled-rights advocate in the world at large. He maintained as hectic a travel schedule as any able-bodied person, even traveling internationally, and he understood how disabilities could affect one's life and self-esteem. Although he had not been disabled as a child, Hawking said, "It is very important that disabled children should be helped to blend with others of the same age. It determines their self-image." Having the right equipment and physical access to buildings and transportation were necessary for a person's feeling of freedom and independence, he believed, but he argued that the attitude of the person was just as important. "It is no use complaining about the public's attitude about the disabled," he said. "It is up to disabled people to change people's awareness in the same way that blacks and women have changed public perceptions." In 1979, as a result of Hawking's efforts to increase the rights of disabled people, the Royal Association for Disability and Rehabilitation honored him with their award for Man of the Year.

During this period, the Hawkings realized that they required the help of professional nurses rather than just the graduate assistants whom they had been relying on. Financially, they were a bit more secure because of Hawking's promotions and the monetary awards that accompanied many of the prizes he received. Jane Hawking, who had gone back to school a few years earlier, had by now finished her doctorate degree in medieval languages and had begun teaching. With their additional income, the Hawkings were able to hire private nurses for a few hours each day. This financial stability, however, would not last for long. With the combination of the educational needs of their growing children and the ever-increasing amount of nursing care Hawking required, the financial strain on the couple loomed large.

In 1982, Hawking decided he would write a popular book on cosmology to help defray the costs of his nursing care and his children's education.

7

A Brief History
of Time

THE FINANCIAL PRESSURES on the Hawkings increased as the 1980s progressed. Their oldest son, Robert, was attending a private school and would soon be heading off to college. Lucy, their daughter, was in a free school, but they wanted to enroll her in the private school that her brother attended. Hawking himself needed more nursing care than the few hours per day that the family could afford. He also knew that if anything were to happen to him, the family would be in dire financial straits because he, as a person who had been expected to die 20 years earlier, had never been able to obtain life insurance. He needed to earn enough money to fund his children's education and to ensure that the family could afford private home care for him rather than being forced to put him in a nursing home should he become incapacitated.

79

In 1982, Hawking hit upon the solution to his financial problem. He decided to write a popular book on cosmology, one meant for mass audiences rather than professional scientists. By early 1983, he was discussing the idea with Simon Mitton, his editor at Cambridge University Press. Because of Hawking's international renown and Cambridge University Press's past success in publishing popular science books, Mitton agreed that it was an excellent idea and told him to go ahead with the book.

Hawking began writing a draft and, when he completed one section, brought it to Mitton. The editor, who had extensive experience writing for the nonscientific market, informed Hawking that his writing was much too technical and scientific for the type of popular book he wanted. Hawking continued to work on the manuscript and then returned to Mitton's office with the edited version. As Mitton read the new version, Hawking sat impassively across from him, watching carefully. Finally, Mitton looked up and told Hawking that the draft was still much too technical. "Look at it this way," he said. "Every equation will halve your sales."

Having spent his entire life dealing with mathematics, Hawking was taken aback by this statement. He did not understand the confusion, dread, or sheer boredom that many people feel when faced with equations. He asked Mitton why he thought that the mathematics would reduce the sales so drastically. The editor explained that when potential buyers pick up a book in a store, they quickly flip through it. "You've got equations on practically every page," he continued. "When they look at this, they'll say, 'This book's got sums in it,' and put it back on the shelf."

Hawking greatly respected Mitton's experience, and he realized that Mitton was right. Hawking knew that if the average person was ever going to be able to understand the book, he would have to make it much simpler. Before he spent more time on it, however, Hawking wanted to agree on the financial terms of the book's publication.

After negotiating for the rest of the afternoon, the two men finally agreed on a large advance and favorable royalties. Although Mitton sent the contract the next day, Hawking never signed it because a more lucrative opportunity intervened.

A January 1983 cover story of the *New York Times Magazine* was an article entitled "The Universe and Dr. Hawking." The story discussed Hawking's many breakthroughs in the research on black holes and cosmology as well as his courageous struggle with ALS. A young editor named Peter Guzzardi saw the story and became fascinated by Hawking. He was intrigued by the idea of a brilliant man who was trapped inside a useless body but was nevertheless making momentous discoveries about the universe. Later that day, Guzzardi discussed Hawking with Al Zuckerman, a literary agent. Zuckerman agreed that a book by Hawking could be very successful.

Zuckerman quickly went to work, contacting Hawking in Cambridge. When Hawking heard from Zuckerman, he was on the verge of signing the contract with Cambridge University Press. Zuckerman explained to Hawking that the sales of the book would be much higher if it was handled by a publisher whose forte was the popular market. Although Cambridge University Press had some experience with popular books, it was primarily an academic publisher and therefore not really appropriate for what Hawking had in mind. Zuckerman persuaded Hawking to delay signing the Cambridge University Press contract. If Zuckerman could not get a better deal from another publisher, Hawking could always return to the original contract.

Hawking wrote a proposal for the book and a sample section that Zuckerman sent out to a number of publishers. Zuckerman told the publishers that if they were interested, they would have to respond with an offer for an advance by a specified date, at which time he would auction off the rights to publish Hawking's book. On the day of the auction, offers inundated Zuckerman's office. By the end of the day, the two companies still in the running were Norton, a highly respected New York publisher that had been very successful at publishing other popular science books, and Bantam, Peter Guzzardi's employer, also situated in New York. By evening, Guzzardi's bosses at Bantam gave him permission to offer Hawking a $250,000 advance against royalties. Norton was unwilling to match the offer, and Bantam purchased the rights to publish Hawking's book.

Shortly thereafter, Hawking and Guzzardi began to work on the manuscript. Hawking sent drafts of sections to Guzzardi in New York and Guzzardi returned them to Hawking filled with comments and suggestions. Not having a scientific background, Guzzardi was the ideal "test" reader. His main goal was to get Hawking to be clear and explicit in his explanations of scientific concepts and the connections between them. "I was persistent," Guzzardi said, "and kept on until Hawking made me understand things. He may have thought I was a little thick, but I risked it and kept on plugging away until I saw what he was talking about." By the time the manuscript was complete, Guzzardi had written at least two pages of letters for each page of manuscript, trying to get Hawking to further amplify and simplify complicated ideas for every page of text that Hawking wrote. After a year and a half, by the summer of 1985, the manuscript was nearly complete. But then disaster struck.

In 1985, while Jane Hawking was vacationing in Germany with some friends, Hawking spent the summer in Geneva, Switzerland, where he could continue with his research and revise the book. Hawking was staying in an apartment with his nurse and research assistant. Late one August night, the nurse entered Hawking's room to check on him and found that he was having difficulty breathing. His face had turned purple and he was making gurgling noises. An ambulance was summoned immediately.

At the hospital, Hawking was put on a ventilator and rushed into intensive care. The doctors concluded that his windpipe was blocked and that he had most likely contracted pneumonia, a disease that often kills ALS patients. Because Jane Hawking was traveling, the doctors had difficulty tracking her down, but they finally found her and told her about her husband's condition.

When Jane Hawking arrived in Geneva, the doctors explained to her that her husband would have little chance of survival if they did not perform a tracheostomy. The operation involved cutting open Hawking's windpipe and implanting a breathing device. He would probably die if the doctors did not perform the operation. Furthermore, the tracheostomy itself would have dire consequences because it would forever prevent Hawking from making any sort of vocal sound. Jane Hawking struggled with the decision she had to make. Although recently only a close circle of friends had been able to understand his speech, Hawking, who had already lost the use of his hands, was still able to communicate verbally. If the doctors performed the operation, he might very well be left completely isolated and unable to communicate at all. After much agonizing, Jane Hawking decided that they must go ahead with the operation. At least then her husband might still live.

Two weeks after the operation, Hawking was flown back to Cambridge and put in intensive care at a hospital there. Although he gradually grew stronger, he had no way of communicating with the nurses. Some of his graduate students and others took turns staying with him in the hospital, so that he had friends nearby around the clock. Although they had no real method of communication either, at least they knew Hawking and had a better idea of what he wanted. Eventually, someone found a mechanism by which Hawking could spell out words. The simple device was a piece of clear plastic out of which all of the letters of the alphabet had been cut. Whoever tried to talk to Hawking held the device up in front of him and looked at Hawking through a large hole in the middle. Hawking then looked at the first letter of the word he was trying to spell, and the other person watched his eyes and guessed which letter he was staring at. If the person guessed the correct letter, Hawking raised his eyebrows as a "yes."

Hawking selects words off a computer monitor during a meeting in Chicago in 1986. After his August 1985 tracheostomy, Hawking was able to communicate with the aid of a computer that had a voice synthesizer.

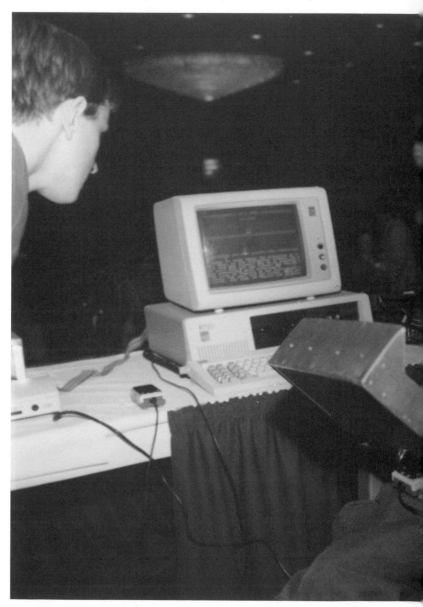

Hawking went home from the hospital after a few weeks, but his family's troubles were far from over. He now required 24-hour nursing care. The National Health Service, Great Britain's state-assisted and state-controlled medical program, could only offer a few hours of private

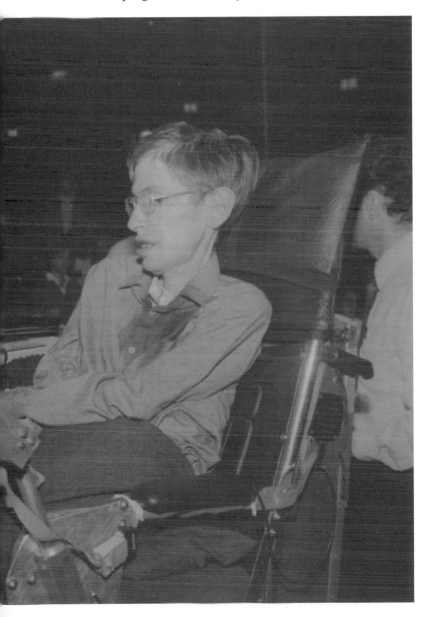

nursing care per week. If Hawking had entered a nursing home, the government would have paid for his care there, but the family was unwilling to send him away because they were sure that it would induce an inevitable physical decline. Paying for private nursing themselves was prohibitively expensive. Even the large advance from Bantam would disappear quickly if the Hawkings had to foot the bill for a nurse's care. In desperation, Jane Hawking wrote to charitable organizations, hoping that one of them might be willing to help. Finally, an American foundation responded with an offer of 50,000 British pounds per year for nursing costs. A few other organizations also made donations. The money enabled the Hawkings to continue living together as a family, but the experience left them embittered. They realized how privileged they were. Had it not been for Hawking's fame, they would have had to put him in a nursing home.

Hawking's worldwide renown helped him in another way. Walt Woltosz, a computer expert in California, heard about Hawking's plight and sent him a copy of a computer program he had written called Equalizer (also referred to as Living Center), which allowed Hawking to select words from a computer monitor. By merely pressing a switch in his hand, Hawking could choose words from a series of menus. If Hawking's physical condition deteriorated even further, the switch could be controlled with a nod of his head or the blink of an eye. When Hawking had built up a sentence or two, he could then send them to a voice synthesizer that would speak the words for him.

With the help of the Equalizer program, Hawking was able to talk again. When he first got the equipment, however, he was reluctant to use it. By using a computer-generated voice, he was acknowledging that he would never be able to use his own voice to speak again. For Hawking, this was a terrible defeat. He soon realized, though, that if he was going to continue with his research and complete his book, he had to use the computer. One of his graduate students, Brian Whitt, remembers the first time that Hawking asked to be helped out of bed so that he could use the computer. After typing "hello," the first thing he typed was, "Will you help me finish my book?"

Although Hawking was still too ill to work, he began to practice with the computer. He soon was able to click on 10 words per minute. "It was a bit slow," he commented, "but then I think slowly, so it suited me quite well." Since then, his years of experience have made him more proficient at using the computer. He can now produce about 15 words per minute. The computer program contains more than 3,000 words in its menus, including some common phrases and complete sentences. After Hawking builds up sentences or paragraphs, he chooses whether to have them spoken out loud or over a telephone line, or stored onto a computer disk. For the first time in years, he could compose his own papers rather than dictate them to someone else. If he has to use equations in his work, he indicates them in words that the computer then transforms into symbols.

The most liberating feature of the program was that it gave Hawking the ability to speak again. Before the operation, only a few very close associates could understand his slurred voice. Now, for the first time in 15 years, everyone—even strangers—could understand what he was saying. No longer did he need to have interpreters to carry on conversations. Nor was his new synthesized voice robotlike. Although Hawking cannot vary the emotion in the voice, it does have intonations. For Hawking, the main drawback of the voice is that it has an American accent. He would, of course, prefer a British one. Nevertheless, a clear voice, whatever the accent, commands the respect that slurred speech does not. Many people assume that slurred speech is a sign of mental as well as physical impairment. Hawking was certainly aware of this misconception, having seen people who stared at his slumped body and reacted to his incomprehensible speech, giving

When delivering a lecture, Hawking has his voice synthesizer plugged into the public address system of the lecture hall; the voice synthesizer reads the computer disk that Hawking has prepared beforehand. Using the computer, it can take a whole day for Hawking to write a 10-page lecture.

the impression that they thought he was some pitiful, mentally deficient creature.

But his new voice was strong and clear. He could now both write and deliver lectures. Even with the computer, however, writing lectures is a time-consuming process for Hawking. It takes him an entire day to write a 10-page

lecture. But after writing it onto a disk and using his voice
synthesizer, he can listen to the lecture himself and then
edit it. To deliver a lecture, his voice synthesizer is plugged
into the public-address system of the lecture hall. As his
disembodied voice reads back the lecture, Hawking sits in
his wheelchair on the stage. When the speech is over, he

asks for questions. Often it takes him 10 minutes to compose an answer, during which time, he tells the audience, "please talk among yourselves, read newspapers, relax." When he has finished writing his reply, he sends it to the voice synthesizer, which then speaks it, and he moves on to the next question. The whole process is so slow that there is little possibility of any dialogue or give-and-take between him and the audience. Some people have commented that listening to a Hawking lecture is a rather surreal experience. Because it is not possible to converse with him in the usual manner, he becomes something of an oracle, forcing students to try to discern the meaning of his statements.

With his newfound strength and the freedom provided by his computer, Hawking began editing the manuscript with Peter Guzzardi again. Hawking worked closely with Brian Whitt to try to make the concepts clearer. They invented analogies that would allow the reader to visualize the idea without compromising the theory behind it. Although the manuscript was now much more readable than it had been originally, Hawking still thought it might be a good idea to include an appendix of the equations that proved the theories. Guzzardi refused to budge from his opinion that, even if they were relegated to an appendix, the equations would intimidate the average reader. Hawking finally deferred to Guzzardi and when the book was published, it had only one equation: Einstein's $E = mc^2$.

Hawking's book *A Brief History of Time: From the Big Bang to Black Holes* was finally published in April 1988. Bantam Books, known for its aggressive marketing campaigns, decided instead to promote the book in a very subdued way. Rather than saturating bookstores with posters and window displays, the publisher decided to let the book sell itself. Although bookstores had shown considerable interest in Hawking's book in their prepublication orders, many of them did not even know in which section they were going to shelve it. The initial publication run was 40,000 copies. A few days after publication, after the books had already been sent to the stores, an editor noticed that two of the book's pictures were in the wrong place. Bantam decided to recall the book. But when Bantam staff members began calling the large bookstores to notify them of the recall, they were amazed to discover that the stores had already sold out their stock. Many bookstores had already reordered the book. Bantam quickly corrected Hawking's book and ordered a large reprinting. As posi-

Hawking's A Brief History of Time: From the Big Bang to Black Holes *was finally published by Bantam Books in 1988. Hawking wrote the cosmology book to be read by scientists and nonscientists alike. It became a best-seller in the United States and in Great Britain.*

tive reviews of *A Brief History of Time* streamed in, the book climbed up the best-seller list and soon reached number one. By summer, the book had already sold half a million copies in the United States alone.

The same sales pattern occurred with the British edition of *A Brief History of Time*. Within days, it was impossible to find a copy of the book in any store in London. In England, it quickly went to the top of the best-seller list and three years later, it remained in the top 10. By January 1992, less than four years after its initial publication, Hawking's book had been translated into 30 languages and had sold 5.5 million copies throughout the world. Stephen Hawking has calculated that this means there is one copy for every 970 people in the world.

Theories abound as to the reasons for the book's success. Hawking wrote the book hoping that people of every occupation and educational background would read it. He did not intend it to be read only by students of science. With so many copies sold, he was obviously successful in his attempt to reach as many readers as possible. Many observers suggested that it became a cult book with which people wanted to be seen. These commentators claim that most of those who own *A Brief History of Time* have not actually read it, nor would they be able to understand it. Some buyers have acknowledged that they never read past the first few pages or that they can only read a single page each day. It has been suggested that by merely being seen with Hawking's book, people believe that they look intelligent and give others the feeling that they are in the presence of knowledge.

Others contend that Hawking's disability has contributed to the book's success. The cover of the American edition has a color photograph of Hawking sitting in his wheelchair against a background of stars. Some critics claimed that by showing his disability, Bantam was exploiting him, trying to make him seem like a poignantly crippled genius. Peter Guzzardi's response to this criticism was to comment that Hawking was a man with a great force of personality, not one who could be easily exploited. Instead, Guzzardi said, "It was a triumph for a man in Hawking's physical condition to be on the cover of his own book. It's inspiring." Hawking himself disliked the photograph, not because it showed him in his wheelchair, but because he thought that the serious frown in the picture was not representative of his personality. Although some of Hawking's fame was undoubtedly due to his having ALS, his scientific achievement had nothing to do with the disease. To have survived as long as Hawking has is a classic tale of a man overcoming the odds; however, this inspiring story alone was not enough to explain the book's phenomenal success.

When *A Brief History of Time* was still on the best-seller list in Britain three years after its publication, an article appeared in the British magazine the *Independent,* pondering the book's popularity and asking for possible explanations from readers. Isobel Hawking wrote a reply, saying that part of the reason for the success of her son's book is that it was so well written. "The ideas are difficult, not the language," she wrote. She also noted that Hawking believes that the concepts he presented are understandable by anyone who is interested in them. Thus, he never adopted an arrogant tone or talked down to his readers. Later, Isobel Hawking would say, "He believes that anyone can understand it. He believes that I can. I think that's a bit optimistic. But he does really believe it." Although his mother read the entire book, she thinks that her non-comprehension of it is due to her educational background rather than to the book itself.

Isobel Hawking's background was similar to many of those curious about the book's success. Like many people who are considered "intellectuals," she had a liberal arts education. Many people interested in literature or history claim to understand nothing about scientific matters, or consider science to be a mechanical pursuit not worthy of

Hawking is seen here in 1990 teaching a class. Many of Hawking's colleagues questioned whether a physicist of his stature should have wasted such valuable research time in writing a mass-market book.

intellectuals. Others, however, acknowledge that there are different types of intelligence. For many people, understanding science is much easier than understanding concepts in the liberal arts. These people would have a much easier time understanding Hawking's book than would the columnists who were questioning its success.

In the scientific community, there were many different opinions about the book and its popularity. Many scientists asked whether a physicist of Hawking's stature should be "wasting his valuable research time" writing a popular book. They did not think it was an important enough endeavor to have so much of his attention. Others thought that, even though it was a very complicated book for nonscientists, it was not thorough enough and that it should have been twice as long. Another criticism was that Hawking should have more clearly distinguished between his own theories and established scientific concepts. The critics complained that he so intermingled the two that a reader without a scientific background would probably not be able to differentiate the two.

For whatever reason, the book was a phenomenal success. No one, including Hawking himself, had ever imagined that it would sell so well. Clearly, Hawking's attempt to make the profound issues of cosmology interesting and accessible to large numbers of people was a great triumph. The book gave Hawking the financial security that he required while firmly establishing his reputation as the most famous living scientist in the world. Unfortunately, this fame would come to haunt him in the future.

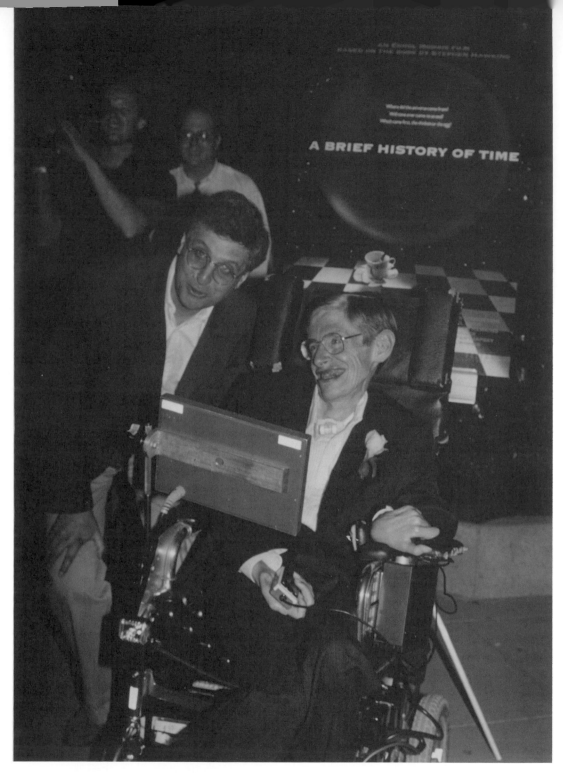

On August 14, 1992, Hawking arrives at the Academy of Motion Picture Arts and Sciences in Beverly Hills, California, for the premiere of the film based on his book A Brief History of Time. *At left is Errol Morris, the director of the film.*

8

FAME AND CONTROVERSY

IF STEPHEN HAWKING was not already the brightest star at Cambridge, the publication and success of *A Brief History of Time* made him so. He became a media darling. He was besieged by requests for interviews from newspapers, magazines, and television shows the world over. A new British documentary about his life and work had filmed him entering King's College in Cambridge. Many viewers must have assumed that he taught at King's College, because after the program aired, the college received a huge increase in requests for admission to study mathematics there. Although Hawking had traveled extensively throughout his professional career, invitations for him to give lectures now flooded in. He accepted many of the offers, and flew around the world, receiving lavish amounts of attention and adulation.

Awards and accolades continued to pour in. In 1988, Hawking and Roger Penrose were awarded the prestigious Wolf Foundation Prize in physics for their work on black holes. Hawking traveled to Jerusalem, Israel, to receive the award and the accompanying $100,000 cash prize. The following year, at Buckingham Palace, Queen Elizabeth II made Hawking a companion of honour—one of Great Britain's most celebrated tributes to men and women who have distinguished themselves in national service and in the advancement of culture. During the same week, he was made an honorary doctor of science by Cambridge University. Only on very rare occasions do universities give honorary awards to their own professors. Prince Philip presented the award to Hawking at a special ceremony. Another event that contributed toward Hawking's being recognized as a national hero and an international celebrity occurred when Lon-

In Jerusalem, Israel's president (far right) and education minister (center) congratulate Hawking for winning the Wolf Foundation Prize in physics on May 12, 1988. The Wolf Foundation Prize is the Israeli equivalent of the Nobel Prize.

don's National Portrait Gallery installed a painting of Hawking in its collection.

Shortly after the publication of *A Brief History of Time,* an American named Gordon Freedman bought the film rights to the book. Freedman contacted David Hickman at Anglia Television in England, and the two agreed to produce a film together. What they had in mind was a movie that would treat both Hawking's life and work, but that would differ from other documentaries in that it would use many graphic representations to explain the scientific concepts. Before they could make the film, however, they needed to find someone to finance the project. They spent the next year trying to raise enough money in England to fund the film. They eventually grew frustrated, and Freedman decided to approach some Americans for assistance. His first thought was to talk to Steven Spielberg, the former "whiz kid" of Hollywood who had made such science-fiction blockbusters as *E.T.* and *Close Encounters of the Third Kind.* Spielberg had a lifelong interest in outer space and had enjoyed reading Hawking's book. He soon agreed to join the project and because of his involvement, the producers had no trouble raising sufficient money for the film.

Next, Freedman and Hickman hired Errol Morris to direct the movie. Morris had made a name for himself in 1988 with *The Thin Blue Line*, an award-winning documentary about a man who was wrongly imprisoned for the killing of a police officer. The movie caused the case to be reopened, eventually resulting in the innocent man's release from prison. For this new project, Morris envisioned a film built around interviews with Hawking's friends, family, and colleagues. When people working on the film began contacting potential interviewees, however, they were surprised to find that many of them were not interested in participating in the project.

Many scientists had not approved of Hawking's decision to write a popular book on cosmology. They thought that in order to make the general public understand such complex scientific concepts the concepts would be over-simplified and thus would lose all meaning. Within the limited format of a movie, these scientists thought, the potential for misrepresentation of the ideas would be even greater. Others felt that a commercial film about Hawking's work would belittle the serious academic atmosphere of Cambridge. Still others had grown envious or resentful of Hawking's fame and were not interested in being involved in another paean to him.

There were people willing to participate, however, and over the course of 13 days Robert Berman, Dennis Sciama, Kip Thorne, Isobel Hawking, and a stream of others sat down to be interviewed. Morris let them talk about whatever they wanted. He often asked them to tell some stories about Hawking, out of which developed some very insightful comments. Morris also interviewed Hawking extensively. He filmed Hawking against a blue screen, a technique used in cinema that enables the image to be projected against any background. Morris noted that by using the blue-screen technique, he was able to "place Stephen Hawking where he belongs, in a mental landscape rather than a real one."

When putting the movie together, Morris intermixed the interviews with simple yet evocative images that were meant to elucidate the scientific concepts. Examples included watches floating through space and broken teacups reassembling themselves. The film was released at the end of 1991 to good reviews. Many critics noted, however, that it was more biographical than scientific in content. This aspect had disturbed Hawking as well, but the filmmakers convinced him that it was necessary to present the details of his life in order to draw people into the theater. Given this constraint, Hawking believed that the movie was as true to the book as it could be. David Hickman, the producer, believed that the movie managed to avoid being either a film biography or a standard science documentary.

He saw it as a different sort of film that dealt more with the subjects of time and religion. "The most exciting thing about cosmology," he said, "is the fact that it interfaces metaphysics and conventional science."

Hawking's fame and success did not come without some controversy. When Hawking had visited Moscow in 1981, his friend Andrei Linde had told him about his latest findings on the new inflationary theory, which posits a rapid expansion of the universe in the first fraction of a second after the big bang. Upon returning to the United States, Hawking went to a seminar in Philadelphia, where, he later claimed in *A Brief History of Time,* he mentioned Linde's ideas. In the Philadelphia audience that day was Paul Steinhardt, a young physicist from the University of Pennsylvania who later published a paper that contained concepts that were very similar to Linde's.

In 1982, Steinhardt learned that Hawking was suggesting that Steinhardt should not get credit for the inflationary model because Hawking had mentioned Linde's work to him at the seminar. In order to defend himself from Hawking's charges of scientific plagiarism, Steinhardt sent Hawking notes and correspondence showing that he had already been working on his inflationary theory months before Hawking's seminar. Moreover, he claimed, he was quite sure that Hawking never mentioned Linde's theories in his lecture. Hawking responded by saying that he accepted Steinhardt's assertion that he had developed his theories independently of Linde's. Steinhardt thought that the dispute was over.

In *A Brief History of Time,* however, Hawking reverted to his position that he had mentioned Linde's inflationary theory to Steinhardt. When Steinhardt saw that section of Hawking's book, he was outraged. Not only was he insulted, but having someone of Hawking's stature criticize a younger scientist such as himself could seriously damage his career. The section in Hawking's book had, in fact, been pointed out to Steinhardt by an employee of the

In March 1989, Hawking and his wife, Jane, hold a press conference in Paris, France, to promote A Brief History of Time. *During the summer of 1990 the Hawkings separated after 25 years of marriage.*

National Science Foundation when Steinhardt had applied for a grant from the foundation. Charges like this could ruin his scientific reputation. Steinhardt again searched through his notes to find verification that his work on the theory predated Hawking's lecture. What he found was something far more conclusive: a videotape of the seminar that he felt would vindicate him once and for all.

He sent the tape to Hawking, who eventually wrote back to say that the section mentioning Steinhardt would be removed from new editions of the book. But Hawking still did not apologize. Finally, after the urging of a mutual friend, Hawking wrote a letter to *Physics Today*, which then published the letter. Hawking had written that he believed Steinhardt had developed his theories independently and he was sorry if he had implied otherwise. Although everyone agrees that Hawking was simply trying to give Linde the credit he thought his friend deserved, his behavior left a sour taste in many people's mouths. This time Hawking's stubbornness, which had often served him so well, seemed to have prevailed over his sense of fairness.

At the same time that this conflict ended, however, trouble was brewing on a more personal front. In the summer of 1990, after being married for 25 years, Stephen and Jane Hawking separated. For weeks, the British tabloids were full of lurid headlines about their breakup. All of Cambridge was shocked by the news. The Hawkings had been at the center of the university's social scene for as long as anyone could remember. Although Jane Hawking had often complained of feeling isolated and ignored while her husband's prizes mounted, the Hawkings had grown even further apart in recent years. Jane Hawking had traveled with her husband less and less on his numerous foreign trips. Hawking had also grown increasingly close to Elaine Mason, his nurse. When he moved out of the house, he moved in with Mason. Although Hawking was the one who had left, he was saddened by the separation. Many people around his office noticed that he very seldom smiled. Whereas in the past he had been the life of the party, he now often seemed depressed, casting a pall over the DAMTP.

As rumors proliferated about the reason for their breakup, both of the Hawkings adamantly refused to discuss their private lives. For many years, however, there had been tensions between them over the subject of religion. Jane Hawking had always been a very religious person. She had often credited the optimism that she derived from her faith in God with allowing her to marry Hawking in the first place and to put so much of herself into caring for him throughout the years. Although they had always held different religious views, as the years passed, increasingly Jane Hawking had the feeling that in his work, her husband was trying to eliminate the need for God. She felt he believed that "because everything is reduced to a rational, mathematical formula, that must be the truth. He is delving into realms that really do matter to thinking people and in a way that can have a very disturbing effect." With Hawking's development of the no boundary model of the universe, he had proposed a view that he felt eliminated the need for a creator. By the bitter end of their relationship, she said she felt that her role was no

Hawking is seen here racing around the campus of Cambridge University. People have always been astonished by Hawking's ability to overcome physical obstacles.

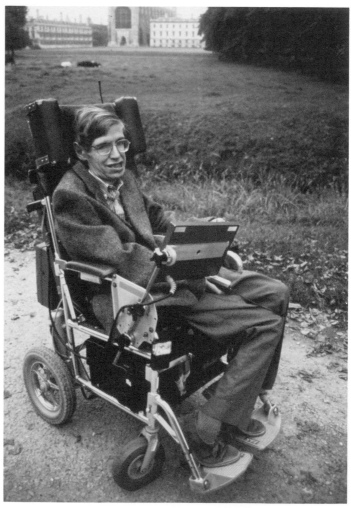

longer that of a nurturing wife ministering to a sick husband, but "simply to tell him that he's not God."

Throughout this difficult period, Hawking continued to
push forward, to do his research, and to live life to the
fullest. He still barreled around Cambridge in his wheelchair. In the spring of 1991, he was driving the wheelchair
at full speed when he approached a road. Thinking that he
could cross the road before the arrival of an oncoming car,
he darted into the street. The car struck his wheelchair,
hurling him onto the pavement and breaking his arm. In
the accident, Hawking cut his head; his wheelchair was
destroyed and his computer was damaged. Two days later,
however, he returned to work.

People have always marveled at Hawking's ability to
overcome physical problems. Many believe that, far from
harming Hawking's career, being stricken with ALS has
helped him focus on theoretical physics. Before he became
ill, he was unmotivated and bored with life. Knowing that
he might die soon made him appreciate life. He has, of
course, been very frustrated by his inability to communicate easily with his colleagues. He must read scientific
papers very slowly because he cannot refer back to them
at will. He cannot simply ask one of his fellow scientists
to clarify an idea, nor can he explain something to them
without it taking a considerable amount of time. But instead of driving him into isolation, this process has imbued
his speech and writing with a succinctness, an elegance,
and a precision that is highly beneficial to him as a
scientist.

Because he is unable to do many activities, whether they
are professorial administrative duties or housework, he has
had much more time to sit and think intensely about
physics, the primary activity of the theoretical physicist.
Hawking's mother believes that his interests were so var-
ied that if Hawking had not become ill, he would not have
concentrated on physics in the way that he has. "I can't say
anyone's lucky to have an illness like that," she has said,

Hawking appears as a guest on the TV series "Star Trek: The Next Generation" in April 1993. The episode filmed here is a scene in which the character Data (back to camera) plays poker on the holodeck with distinguished scientists (from left to right) Albert Einstein, Hawking, and Sir Isaac Newton.

"but it's less bad luck for him than it would be for some people, because he can so much live in his head." Some people also believe that having this type of disability makes one more introspective, an advantage in a field of work that takes place almost entirely in a theoretical realm. Because Hawking has to do everything in his head, he has also tended to search for explanations that are simpler, those that do not require extensive calculations. In physics, these simple, elegant explanations are considered the ideal.

Isobel Hawking said of her son, "He does believe very intensely in the almost infinite possibility of the human mind. . . . He's a searcher, he is looking for things. And if sometimes he may talk nonsense, well, don't we all? The point is, people must think, they must go on thinking, they must try to extend the boundaries of knowledge."

Hawking has continued to do just that. In the 30 years since he was told by doctors that he had two years to live, he has vastly extended humankind's understanding of the universe and its origins. He also made this knowledge accessible to the general public in 1988 by writing *A Brief History of Time*. In 1993, Hawking published a compilation of 13 essays, autobiographical and scientific in content, including an interview he had with the British Broadcasting Corporation, entitled *Black Holes and Baby Universes and Other Essays*. Through his books, he has awakened in many people a fascination with science and a curiosity about the universe. Although he now doubts that the Theory of Everything will be discovered by the year 2000, he still believes it is on the horizon, and he remains one of the small group of brilliant physicists who is most likely to discover it. For Hawking, it is the only interesting question. "My goal," he once said, "is a complete understanding of the universe, why it is as it is and why it exists at all."

FURTHER READING

Boslough, John. *Stephen Hawking's Universe.* New York: William Morrow, 1985.

Ferguson, Kitty. *Stephen Hawking: Quest for a Theory of the Universe.* New York: Franklin Watts, 1991.

Hawking, Stephen W. *Black Holes and Baby Universes and Other Essays.* New York: Bantam, 1993.

———. *A Brief History of Time: From the Big Bang to Black Holes.* New York: Bantam, 1988.

———, ed. *Stephen Hawking's A Brief History of Time: A Reader's Companion.* Prepared by Gene Stone. New York: Bantam, 1992.

Lightman, Alan, and Roberta Brawer. *Origins: The Lives and Worlds of Modern Cosmologists.* Cambridge, MA: Harvard University Press, 1990.

Overbye, Dennis. *Lonely Hearts of the Cosmos: The Scientific Quest for the Secret of the Universe.* New York: HarperCollins, 1991.

Simon, Sheridan. *Stephen Hawking: Unlocking the Universe.* Minneapolis: Dillon, 1991.

White, Michael, and John Gribbin. *Stephen Hawking: A Life in Science.* New York: Dutton, 1992.

Chronology

INDEX

Melissa McDaniel, a native of Portland, Oregon, received her B.A. in history from Portland State University and her M.L.S. from the University of Washington. A former librarian, she is presently a freelance writer living in New York City.

Jerry Lewis is the National Chairman of the Muscular Dystrophy Association (MDA) and host of the MDA Labor Day Telethon. An internationally acclaimed comedian, Lewis began his entertainment career in New York and then performed in a comedy team with singer and actor Dean Martin from 1946 to 1956. Lewis has appeared in many films—including *The Delicate Delinquent, Rock a Bye Baby, The Bellboy, Cinderfella, The Nutty Professor, The Disorderly Orderly,* and *The King of Comedy*—and his comedy performances continue to delight audiences around the world.

John Callahan is a nationally syndicated cartoonist and the author of an illustrated autobiography, *Don't Worry, He Won't Get Far on Foot.* He has also produced three cartoon collections: *Do Not Disturb Any Further, Digesting the Child Within,* and *Do What He Says! He's Crazy!!!* He has recently been the subject of feature articles in the *New York Times Magazine,* the *Los Angeles Times Magazine,* and the Cleveland *Plain Dealer,* and has been profiled on "60 Minutes." Callahan resides in Portland, Oregon.